Word Wizardry for Writers

Wolf O'Rourc

A concise guide to useful features of Microsoft Word for **Windows** and **Mac** for writers of fiction and non-fiction alike.

Don't be a slave to Word, let Word slave for you. Word Wizardry for Writers walks you through the features of the program that allow you to write, format, and publish quicker, so you can focus on your stories, instead of technicalities. Topics include using styles to conform to the needs of self-publishing services, maximizing the power of built-in functions like replace or AutoCorrect, and formatting pages with proper headers and footers. Liberal sprinklings of detailed steps and tips for **Word for Mac 2004** to **2011**, **Word 2003** to **2010**, and an update for **Word 2013**, help you get the most out of your tools-of-the-trade.

Warning: Not suitable as a doorstop.

For Sydnee and Nancy, who nursed this book to life

Edition 1, 2014

My thanks to Sydnee Elliot, Nancy Sansone, Carrie Ann Lahain, and Mike Rausch for technical and content support.

Introduction

Microsoft Word has two or three gazillion functions, more than even ancient and powerful wizards, witches, warlocks, sorcerers, shamans, or other purveyors of magic understand. Seasoned writers wonder in amazement when their sacred texts change in mysterious ways after they place them in the care of Word. To save your sanity, this booklet describes some of the most helpful tools in the Word arsenal to put them quickly at your fingertips in your heroic struggle with the many demands of publishing.

Conventions

Each chapter starts with a general description of some functionality, followed by detailed <u>steps</u> for different versions. If a task can be done in multiple ways, <u>dashed lines</u> separate the different methods. Usage examples round out the chapter.

Five tags highlight important points.

TIP	Tips present noteworthy exceptions or clever uses of a particular function.
BR	The Before Ribbon sections present differences in Office 2003 and earlier versions.
MAC	The Mac sections present differences in Word for Macintosh.
O07	These sections present differences in Office 2007.
O13	These sections present differences in Office 2013.

The text sticks closely to Microsoft wording used in help and on its web site. A recap of some of the most common terms follows.

Click means placing the cursor over text, a button, a menu choice, or some other object and pressing the *left* mouse button.

Right-click means placing the cursor over text or an object and pressing the *right* mouse button.

Control-click means placing the cursor over text or an object, holding down the `[Control]` or `[Ctrl]` key, then pressing the mouse button—an alternative to right-click on the **Mac**.

Select means placing a black or blue highlight over text or objects by dragging with the mouse while holding down a button, or using movement keys while holding down the `[Shift]` key, so the selection can be manipulated by a function. Word specific methods for selecting are discussed in 1.4.

A vertical bar (|), also known as a pipe, separates choices in drop-down menus, the Ribbon, or dialog boxes. Wording used onscreen is shown in bold. For example, the following instructs you to click the **Office Button**, the colorful, round button used instead of the word "Office" in the menu, then click **Word Options** in the next menu.

Click **Office Button | Word Options**.

Buttons in dialog boxes, such as [OK], are indicated by square brackets.

Keyboard use is indicated by a `courier font` and square brackets within text. The plus sign (+) means that you press and hold the first key, then press the second key. Additional plus signs add to the number of keys to hold. For example, to copy the current format to the Format Painter, hold the `[Ctrl]` key and the `[Shift]` key, then press `[C]`.

`[Ctrl] + [Shift] + [C]`

A comma (,) means that you press one key, release it, then press the next key. For example, to select a word, press and release the [F8] key, then press it again.

```
[F8], [F8]
```

The keyboard shortcuts in this book apply to the U.S. keyboard layout. Some shortcuts may differ in other languages. Please refer to the online help or the notes on the Microsoft web site for any differences.

To identify clearly any symbols to include when filling out fields, a box surrounds the text to type in. For example, xe ^? means type lowercase "xe", a space, a circumflex, and a question mark into the field.

WolfORourc.com

Google+

Facebook

Some writers are infallible. I'm not one of them. However, I never make mistakes. Any problems in this book can thus only come from my fingers slipping on the keyboard at two in the morning, or AutoCorrect (see 3.3) changing what I typed to what Microsoft Word felt like. In the super, super unlikely event that you find a teensy, tiny error in this document, please feel free to let me know at one of the addresses below. I promise to expeditiously—meaning within the current year—deal with any reports as I see fit. For your convenience, you can scan the QR codes, instead of typing the addresses.

Technological progress never stops. Microsoft Word moves forward, as does the publishing industry. Check my web site regularly for updates and more helpful tips.

Wolf's Web site: www.WolfORourc.com
Wolf on Facebook: http://www.facebook.com/wolf.orourc
Wolf's Twitter handle: @WolfORourc
Wolf on Google Plus:
https://plus.google.com/u/0/100309131294366685432

Table of Content

Table of Tables

Table of Figures

1. Word Basics

This chapter covers basic Microsoft Word functionality referenced throughout the book, such as the interface, cursor movement, and simple editing functions.

> **TIP** Microsoft provides many instructional articles and videos on using Word on the web site office.microsoft.com.

1.1. The Word Interface

For computers, an interface is the point of interaction between its components, or with the user through peripheral devices such as the monitor or a keyboard. For humans it becomes the de facto face of the device or a program. Considerable thought goes into designing an interface, and changes to it cause much confusion and anguish among longtime users. Word has a number of interfaces currently in use. This subchapter presents the major ones.

1.1.1. Word 2013

Given Office 2013's recent release, this book still focuses on the widely used version 2010 described below. Office 2013 introduces additional collaboration functions such as storing documents in the Internet cloud to make them accessible everywhere. It requires Microsoft Windows 7 or later.

Figure 1-1: Word 2013 Interface

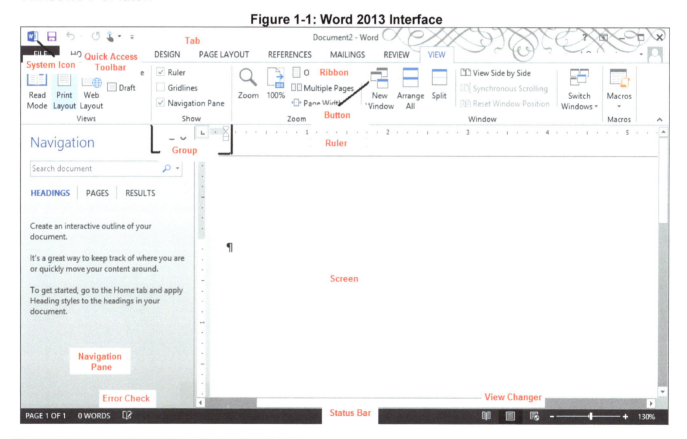

> **O13** Throughout the book sections marked by **O13** point out differences in usage in Office 2013.

The Interface has changed again, but most of the Ribbon remains the same. The **Backstage View** uses tiles similar to Windows 8 for file access. Word 2013 adds improvements for use with touch screens and pens. The Focus View introduced in Word for Mac 2011 evolved into **Read Mode**, an optimized, uncluttered display that allows focusing on reading.

O13   To hide or show the **Ribbon** use the **Ribbon Display Options** button⊞ in the upper right corner.

The **Navigation Pane** combines the search and browse functions similar to the Mac interface (See 1.6).

1.1.2.   Word 2010

For reasons only known to the gods, Microsoft changed to a new results-oriented user interface in Word 2007 named **Office Fluent**. The most noticeable feature is **The Ribbon**, the much feared gigantic bar with buttons going across the top. The Ribbon's tab names and buttons adjust to the context of your work, similar to specialized toolbars popping up in older versions. Since the collection of commands under the Ribbon tabs differs considerably from the old menus, you will find steps for both the 2003 and prior interface, known in this book as "**BR**" or "Before Ribbon," and versions 2007 and later, also known as "**AR**" or "After Ribbon."

TIP   Hovering with the cursor over a command button will display a tool tip, a pop-up bubble explaining the function of the button, including its keyboard shortcut.

TIP   You can customize the Ribbon to move commands that you use often close together. Under **File | Options | Customize Ribbon** you can add buttons, groups, even tabs, remove or rearrange buttons, and change the appearance of the whole Ribbon.

Figure 1-2: Word 2010 Interface

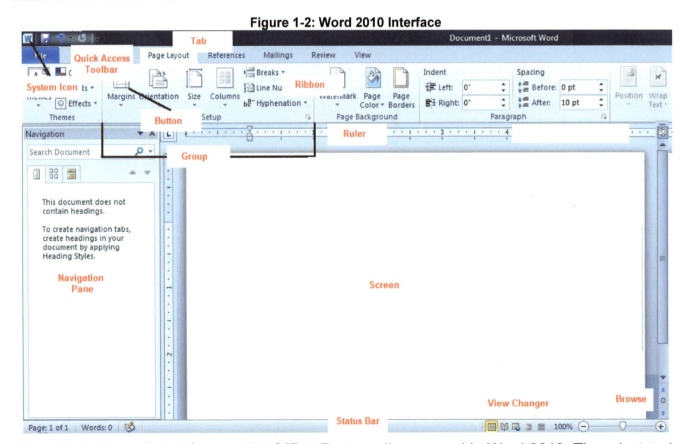

A particularly confusing feature, the **Office Button**, disappeared in Word 2010. The reinstated **File** and **System** menus contain the commands for those tasks. Clicking the **System Icon**🅦, a blue "W," drops the **System** menu containing functions to minimize or close the entire Microsoft Word window. The unmodified version of Word looks like Figure 1-2.

Taking up most of the space above the document window, the **Ribbon** stretches across the screen. Its **Command Buttons** allow executing some of the most common functions in Word, gathered together in logical **Groups** of related activities. The task-oriented **Tabs** above the Ribbon allow selection of the major groupings such as "Insert," tools for inserting objects into the document, or "Page Layout," tasks related to how the page looks overall.

TIP   Pressing the [Alt] key displays the keyboard assignments (KeyTips) for the Ribbon tabs. After picking a tab by pressing a key, the KeyTips for the buttons appear, allowing you to run a command without the mouse.

TIP   Pressing the [Alt] key *and* the shortcut key for the top-level Before Ribbon menu allows you to type the entire **BR** shortcut sequence to run a command without the mouse. For example, [Alt] + [O], [S] opens the **Styles** task pane.

At the very top, next to the **System Icon**, the **Quick Access Toolbar** (QAT) gives access to a set of commands independent of the tab that is currently displayed. Some of the most often used functions, such as save the file, undo, and print appear here.

Figure 1-3: The 2010 Quick Access Toolbar

TIP   You can customize the Quick Access Toolbar to have frequently used commands available all the time. Under **File | Options | Quick Access Toolbar**, add, remove, or rearrange buttons and move the QAT below the Ribbon. The dropdown list on the right allows you to create a Quick Access Toolbar specific to one document, for example, if you want different functions available for editing novels or non-fiction works. The **Customize** *down triangle* ⩔ at the end of the QAT also allows customization.

TIP   To add a function to the Quick Access Toolbar on the fly, right-click the button in the Ribbon and select **Add to Quick Access Toolbar** on the shortcut menu. You can only add commands to the QAT. The *contents* of most lists, such as a single style that appears on the Ribbon, cannot be added individually.

TIP   If you prefer to use the additional screen space, double-click the active tab to temporarily minimize and expand the Ribbon or hit [CTRL] + [F1]. To keep the Ribbon minimized except when you click a tab, click the **Customize Quick Access Toolbar** button then click **Minimize the Ribbon**.

O13   To keep the Ribbon minimized or visible use the up arrow ⌃ or pin ⫝̸ at its lower right.

On the far right, the **View Ruler** button ⊠ displays the horizontal and vertical rulers, the graduated strips that show the dimensions of the document and give you quick access to margins, indentations, and tab settings. The **Tab Selector** button ⌐ on the far left specifies what tab type is placed when you click the horizontal ruler (See 5.2).

Word Wizardry for Writers

> **TIP** To ensure consistency only change paragraph indentations and tab settings when absolutely needed. Change the style settings instead to affect all similar paragraphs in the document. It will make your life easier during the self-publishing process.

The **Navigation Pane**, introduced in Word 2010, permits quick movement to a page or heading. It combines the functions of the **Document Map**, **Find,** and **Go To** dialog boxes in previous versions (See 1.6).

Displaying the Navigation Pane

AR: Click **View** | **Navigation Pane** (Show group).
BR: Click **View** | **Document Map** or **View** | **Thumbnails**.

Click the page count in the status bar.

`[Alt] + [V], [D]`

`[Ctrl] + [F]`

The **Status Bar** at the bottom displays helpful information about the document, like the current page number. Clicking certain areas launches commands. On the right, the **View Changer** provides buttons with the same functions as the **Views** group of the **View** tab (See 1.7). The document text occupies the rest of the window. Microsoft calls this area the **Screen**.

1.1.3. Word for Mac

The features of the **Office Fluent** interface common with Word 2010 are described above under 1.1.2. Unlike the Windows version, Word for Mac 2011 keeps the customary menu bar *and* displays the Ribbon in addition. A typical setup from Office 2011 is shown in Figure 1-4. This version clearly shows the transition from one interface to another. Often the steps for the Ribbon work, while, at times, you still need to use the menu for many functions. Many tasks have a Mac specific command sequence, hence the layout and buttons of the Mac Ribbon differ considerably from the Windows version.

Except for a few functions mentioned in the text, the menus differ little from earlier ones, hence I have omitted separate sections for different Mac versions. Try the Before Ribbon (BR) steps, unless a separate Mac section offers alternatives. In Word 2011 the After Ribbon (AR) steps may work, too.

> **MAC** Throughout the book sections marked by MAC point out differences in usage in Office for Mac.
>
> **MAC** Pressing `[Control] + [F2]` or `[Control] + [Fn] + [F2]` sets the focus to the menu bar. Typing the beginning of a menu choice moves the highlight there and pressing `[Return]` allows you to select a command without the mouse. For example, `[Control] + [F2]`, `[I]`, `[Return]`, `[B]`, `[R]`, `[Return]`, `[Return]` inserts a page break.

Word 2011 introduces the **Focus View**, an uncluttered display that allows focusing on reading.

> **MAC** If your mouse does not allow right-clicking, you can bring up the context-sensitive menus in the text or Ribbon by *control-clicking*, holding down `[Control]` or `[Ctrl]` while clicking the mouse.

Figure 1-4: Word for Mac 2011 Interface

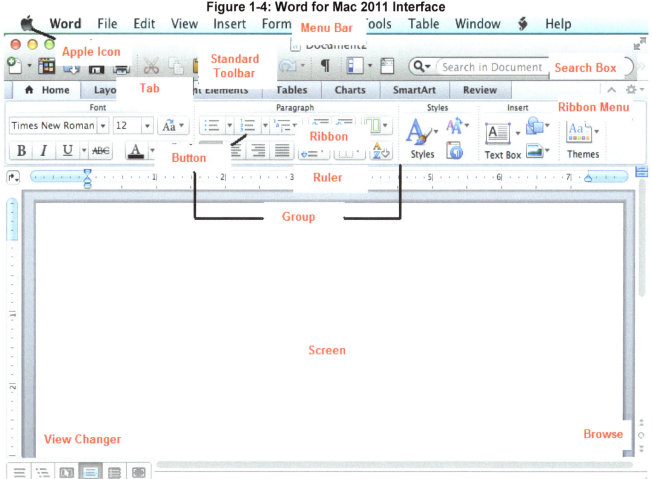

MAC Some Mac keyboards require pressing [Fn] to use function keys. For example, [Shift] + [F5] becomes [Shift] + [Fn] + [F5].

MAC If you prefer to use the additional screen space, minimize the Ribbon under **View** by unchecking **Ribbon** or hit [Cmd] + [Option] + [1] or [Control] + [F1]. Double-clicking the active tab also temporarily minimizes and expands the Ribbon. To turn it off completely, click the **Settings** button ⚙▾ in the Ribbon menu on the right, select **Ribbon Preferences**, then under **General**, clear the **Turn on the ribbon** check box. To turn the Ribbon back on use the menu choice **Word | Preferences | Sharing and Privacy | Ribbon**.

Word 2011 also keeps the customary **Standard Toolbar** that gives access to a set of commands independent of the tab that is currently displayed. Some of the most often used functions, such as save the file, undo, and print appear here.

Figure 1-5: The 2011 Standard Toolbar

MAC You can customize the Standard Toolbar to have frequently used commands available all the time. Right-click or control-click anywhere within the toolbar, then select **Customize Toolbars and Menus**.

MAC	Like most Mac programs Word also lists keyboard shortcuts in its menus. The following symbols represent the modifier keys.
⌘	Command key (🍎 on some keyboards).
^	Control key.
⌥	Option/Alt key.
⇧	Shift key.
Fn	Function key.

The Mac version includes a rudimentary **Navigation Pane**, called the **Sidebar**, for quick movement to a page or heading using the **Thumbnails Pane** and **Document Map**. Word 2011 adds find functions to it.

Displaying the Thumbnails Pane or Document Map Pane

Click **View | Sidebar** or **View | Navigation Pane** then check **Thumbnails Pane** or **Document Map Pane**.

Click **Show or hide the Sidebar** or **Navigation Pane** on the Standard Toolbar, then click the **Thumbnails Pane** or **Document Map** buttons at the top.

1.1.4.   Word 2007

The features of the **Office Fluent** interface used with Word 2007 are described above under 1.1.2. This section highlights some differences to later versions.

Figure 1-6: Word 2007 Interface

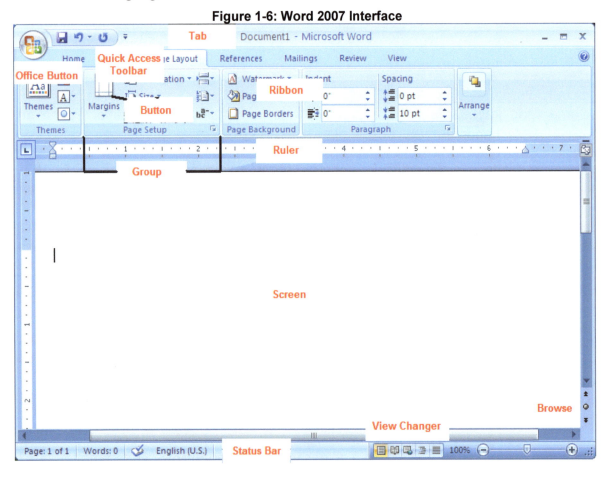

O07 Throughout the book sections marked by O07 point out differences in usage in Office 2007.

 The **Office Button**, the colorful button on the left of the window also known as It-Who-Must-Not-Be-Named, replaced the **File** and **System Menu** in previous versions. The unmodified version of Word 2007 looks like Figure 1-6.

Word 2007 also introduced the **Quick Access Toolbar** (QAT) that gives access to a set of commands independent of the tab that is currently displayed. Some of the most often used functions, such as save the file, undo, and redo appear here.

Figure 1-7: The 2007 Quick Access Toolbar

TIP You can customize the Quick Access Toolbar to have frequently used commands available all the time. Click the **Office** button, then the **Word Options** button, and select **Customize**. Add, remove, or rearrange buttons and move the QAT below the Ribbon. The dropdown list on the right allows you to create a Quick Access Toolbar specific to one document, for example, if you want different functions available for editing novels or non-fiction works. The *down triangle* ⏷ at the end of the QAT also allows customization.

TIP To add a function to the Quick Access Toolbar on the fly, right-click the button in the Ribbon and select **Add to Quick Access Toolbar** on the shortcut menu. You can only add commands to the QAT. The *contents* of most lists, such as a single style that appears on the Ribbon, cannot be added individually.

1.1.5. Word 2003

Before Ribbon Word used the customary interface introduced with Microsoft Windows or the Apple Macintosh composed of a menu bar and customizable toolbars. A typical setup for the last BR version, Office 2003, is shown in Figure 1-8.

Before Ribbon, the **Title Bar** only contained the **System Icon**, a blue "W." When clicked, it drops the **System** menu containing system functions, for example to minimize or close the entire Microsoft Word window.

Below the title bar, the **Menu Bar** holds various menus that group related activities together. Some, like **File** and **Edit**, are common with other applications. Below the menus, various customizable **Toolbars** containing **Buttons** give quick access to frequently used functions.

TIP Hovering with the cursor over a button will display a pop-up bubble with the name of the button.

TIP Pressing the [Alt] key *and* the underlined letter in a top-level menu choice opens that submenu. Typing the underlined letters allows you to select a command without the mouse. For example, [Alt] + [F], [A] opens the **Save As** dialog box.

TIP You can customize the display and content of toolbars to move commands that you use often close together. Under **Tools | Customize** add, remove, or rearrange buttons. Right-clicking the toolbar area also allows you to change its appearance.

Figure 1-8: Word 2003 Interface

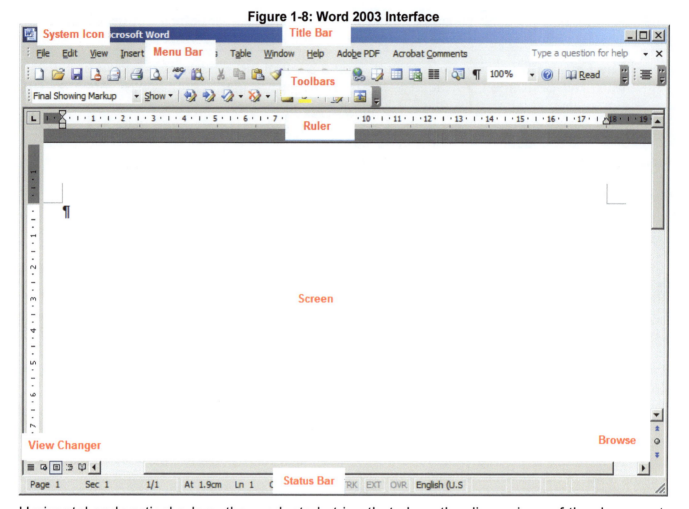

Horizontal and vertical rulers, the graduated strips that show the dimensions of the document, give you quick access to margins, indentations, and tab settings. The **Tab Selector** button ∟ on the far left specifies what tab type is placed when you click the horizontal ruler (See 5.2).

> **TIP**   To ensure consistency only change paragraph indentations and tab settings when absolutely needed. Change the style settings instead to affect all similar paragraphs in the document. It will make your life easier during the self-publishing process.

The **Status Bar** at the bottom displays helpful information about the document, like the current page number. Above it, next to the slider, the **View Changer** provides buttons with the same functions as the top of the **View** menu (See 1.7). The document text occupies the rest of the window. Microsoft calls this area the **Screen**.

1.2.   Text Entry

Obviously, you type text on the keyboard. Occasionally you may need a character missing from the keyboard, such as the copyright symbol (©) or the degree symbol (°) for temperature. This book uses two conventions for keyboard shortcuts. The plus sign (+) means that you press and hold the first key, then press the second key. Additional plus signs add to the number of keys to hold. A comma (,) means that you press one key, release it, then press the next key.

Before we go into special text entries, a word about storage. To a computer, a file is nothing but a sequence of numbers without any special meaning. Programs like Word look at the numbers and decide what to do with the stream. Coding systems like ASCII or ANSI standardize the meaning of these numbers. For example, in both systems the decimal number 65 represents the letter "A" in capital. Some numbers do not display on the screen, but instead format the text. For example, the number 13 represents a carriage return, which tells Word to end the current line and start a new one. Hitting the [Enter] key puts the code 13 into the file. At times, you may want to see the formatting characters, particularly if the display on screen appears off. Word provides a number of methods to make these formatting characters visible on your screen. They do *not* appear on reader's computers, unless they have the same options turned on. Printed documents do not show the formatting characters regardless of the Word settings. The **Show/Hide** button ¶ makes all hidden text visible. Quite an overwhelming experience the first time you see it, but you can selectively choose to display just a few of the most common entries in the View or Display options. The **Show/Hide** button does not affect any marks turned on this way. Figure 1-9 shows the most common formatting marks.

Making formatting characters temporary visible

AR: Click **Home | Show/Hide** ¶ (Paragraph group).
BR/MAC: Click **Show/Hide** ¶ on **Standard toolbar**.

[Ctrl] + [*] (numeric keypad only)

Making formatting characters or hidden text permanently visible

AR: Click **File | Options | Display**.
O07: Click **Office | Word Options | Display**.
BR: Click **Tools | Options | View**.
MAC: Click **Word | Preferences | View**.
Check the boxes for the formatting marks or **Hidden text**.

Figure 1-9: Display options with common formatting marks

Always show these formatting marks on the screen

☐	Tab characters	→
☐	Spaces	...
☐	Paragraph marks	¶
☐	Hidden text	a̶b̶c̶
☐	Optional hyphens	¬
☐	Object anchors	⚓
☑	Show all formatting marks	

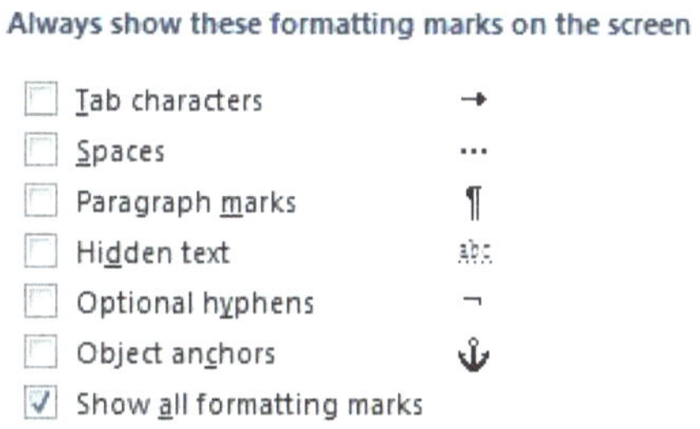

> **TIP**   Hidden text is a great way to hide research in a book. It is available while you write, yet does not appear in print.

If you have more tab characters or leading spaces in one line than another, characters will not line up. To count them precisely, turn the display of formatting marks on. Remove right arrows, the symbol for tabs, or dots, the symbol for spaces, until all lines have the same number.

Entering characters not on the keyboard

AR: Click **Insert | Symbol** (Symbols group) | **More Symbols**.
BR: Click **Insert | Symbol**.

MAC: Click **Insert | Symbol | Symbol Browser** or open the **Media Browser** from the Standard Toolbar and select the **Symbols** tab. To get a similar dialog box as in Figure 1-10 Click **Insert | Symbol | Advanced Symbol**.

In the **Symbol dialog box** select a character from the **Symbols** or the **Special Characters** table.

Click [Insert]

Use the shortcut keys assigned by Word to a symbol.

Use the AutoCorrect equivalent (See 3.3).

Hold down [Alt] and type the ASCII or ANSI code for the character *on the numeric keypad*. This method does not work with the number keys at the top of the keyboard. If the cursor moves instead, hit [NumLk] to turn numbers lock on.

Type the three-digit Unicode number. This method works with the numeric keypad and the number keys at the top.

Alt + X

MAC: [Option] + *letter key*. The **Advanced Symbol** dialog box lists available keyboard shortcuts.

Figure 1-10: Symbol dialog box

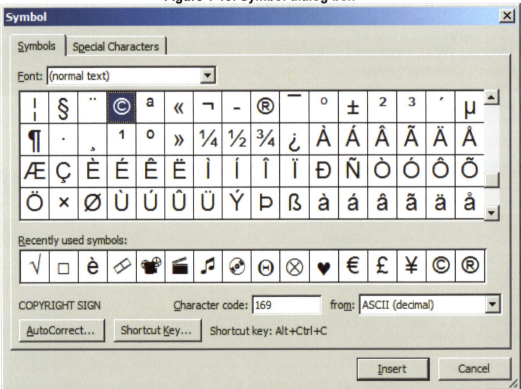

The **Symbol dialog box** shows a table with all characters in the selected font shown in the **Font** box. Clicking a character displays the character code of the font below and any assigned shortcut keys. The [Shortcut Key] button allows you to assign your own keystroke combination to symbols you frequently use.

Figure 1-10 shows the dialog box with the copyright symbol selected. As you can see, the decimal ASCII code is 169. Switching the **from** list to Unicode displays 00A9 instead. To enter the © from the keyboard either use the shortcut [Alt] + [Ctrl] + [C], or hold down

[Alt] and type the decimal ASCII code 169 on a numeric keypad, or type the hexadecimal Unicode 00A9 followed by [Alt] + [X].

The **Special Characters** tab puts frequently used symbols, including ©, at your mouse tip without needing to search the long tables.

1.3. Cursor Movement

Microsoft Word supports the common movement keys of the operating system. These have not changed with the introduction of the Ribbon. The following tables summarize the most commonly used keystrokes for Microsoft Windows and Mac OS.

Table 1-1: Cursor movement keys (Windows)

Home	Move to the beginning of the entry.
End	Move to the end of the entry.
Ctrl + Home	Move to the beginning of the document.
Ctrl + End	Move to the end of the document.
Left Arrow	Move one character to the left.
Right Arrow	Move one character to the right.
Ctrl + Left Arrow	Move one word to the left.
Ctrl + Right Arrow	Move one word to the right.
Down Arrow	Move one line down.
Up Arrow	Move one line up.
Ctrl + Down Arrow	Move one paragraph down.
Ctrl + Up Arrow	Move one paragraph up.
PgDn (Page Down)	Move one screen down.
PgUp (Page Up)	Move one screen up.

Table 1-2: Cursor movement keys (Mac)

Home or Cmd + Left Arrow	Move to the beginning of the entry.
End or Cmd + Right Arrow	Move to the end of the entry.
Cmd + Home or Cmd + Fn + Left Arrow	Move to the beginning of the document.
Cmd + End or Cmd + Fn + Right Arrow	Move to the end of the document.
Left Arrow	Move one character to the left.
Right Arrow	Move one character to the right.
Option + Left Arrow	Move one word to the left.
Option + Right Arrow	Move one word to the right.
Down Arrow	Move one line down.
Up Arrow	Move one line up.
Cmd + Down Arrow	Move one paragraph down.
Cmd + Up Arrow	Move one paragraph up.
Page Down or Fn + Down Arrow	Move one screen down.
Page Up or Fn + Up Arrow	Move one screen up.
Cmd + Page Down or Cmd + Fn + Down Arrow	Move one page down.
Cmd + Page Up or Cmd + Fn + Up Arrow	Move one page up.

These keys apply to both movements within regular text and within a table. For example, hitting [End] within regular text will move the cursor to the end of the line. Within a table, the same keystroke moves to the end of the cell. In the context of movement within Microsoft Word, the word "screen" means the visible text below the menus, toolbars, ribbons, and rulers and above the status bar and sliders. Microsoft also refers to this area as "window."

Word has special functions for moving within a document, as listed in Table 1-9 in the subchapter on Find and Replace. [Shift] + [F5] comes in particularly handy during editing when you need to check something you wrote before. Word keeps track of the last three locations where you typed or edited text. After searching for a passage, you can use the key combination to quickly jump back to the last locations you worked on.

> **TIP**   Some changes do not cause Word to record the location. If [Shift] + [F5] does not work, try **Undo↺** instead. Once Word has returned you to the location of the change, use **Redo** to apply the change again.
>
> **TIP**   After pasting a large block of text, if you want to edit it, use [Shift] + [F5] to return to the beginning of the insertion.

1.4.   Text Selection

Word applies formatting and text-related functions to the highlighted (selected) text. By holding the mouse button while dragging across text, you can select and unselect text. In combination with the [Shift] key the movement keys in 1.3 also extend (select text) or shorten (unselect text) a selection. The highlight normally starts at the current cursor location and changes by the cursor movement. The following table summarizes selection by keyboard.

> **MAC** To select text, use the Mac keyboard combinations from Table 1-2 together with [Shift].

Table 1-3: Text selection keys

Shift + Home	Select to the beginning of the entry.
Shift + End	Select to the end of the entry.
Shift + Ctrl + Home	Select to the beginning of the document.
Shift + Ctrl + End	Select to the end of the document.
Shift + Left Arrow	Select one character to the left.
Shift + Right Arrow	Select one character to the right.
Shift + Ctrl + Left Arrow	Select one word to the left.
Shift + Ctrl + Right Arrow	Select one word to the right.
Shift + Down Arrow	Select one line down.
Shift + Up Arrow	Select one line up.
Shift + Ctrl + Down Arrow	Select to end of paragraph.
Shift + Ctrl + Right Arrow	Select to beginning of paragraph.
Shift + PgDn	Select one screen-full down.
Shift + PgUp	Select one screen-full up.

In some instances, Word adjusts to word and paragraph boundaries. For examples, whereas [Ctrl] + [Down Arrow] moves to the *beginning* of the next paragraph, [Shift] + [Ctrl] + [Down Arrow] selects to the *end* of the current paragraph, including the paragraph mark.

> **TIP**   To view paragraph marks and other formatting symbols, on the **Home** tab, in the Paragraph group, click **Show/Hide** ¶ .

Including the space after a word ensures that the spacing looks correct during cut and paste operations. Including the paragraph mark ensures that the paragraph formatting is also copied to the new location, and that a blank line does not remain at the original location. If Word automatically adjusting spaces and blank lines bothers you, you can change this "smart" behavior.

Stop Word from automatically selecting space at end of word

AR: Click **File | Options | Advanced**.
O07: Click **Office Button | Word Options | Advanced**.
BR: Click **Tools | Options | Edit**.
MAC: Click **Word | Preferences | Edit**.
Under **Editing options**, clear the **When selecting, automatically select entire word** check box.

Stop Word from automatically selecting paragraph mark

AR: Click **File | Options | Advanced**.
O07: Click **Office Button | Word Options | Advanced**.
BR: Click **Tools | Options | Edit**.
MAC: Click **Word | Preferences | Edit**.
Under **Editing options**, clear the **Use smart paragraph selection** (**MAC**: **Include paragraph mark when selecting paragraphs**) check box.

Word provides additional mechanisms for selecting frequently used objects. The cursor keys together with shift, except for the smart feature, do not recognize grammatical building blocks. The `[F8]` key does double duty. If pressed once, it puts Word into extend mode where the movement keys or the mouse will highlight text without the need to hold down shift. If pressed multiple times, it cycles the selection through the basic grammatical building box.

Table 1-4: Special selection keys

`F8`	Turn extend mode on or increase size of selection.
`Esc` (or **MAC** `Cmd + Period`)	Turn extend mode off.
`Shift + F8`	Reduce the size of a selection.
`Ctrl + A` (**MAC**: `Cmd + A`)	Select entire document.

Selecting a word

Double-click anywhere in the word.

`F8, F8`

Selecting a line

Click to the left of the line. (Cursor points to the right)

Selecting a sentence

Hold `[Ctrl]` and **click** anywhere in the sentence.

MAC: Hold `[Cmd]` and **click** anywhere in the sentence.

```
F8, F8, F8
```

Selecting a paragraph

Double-click to the left of the line. (Cursor points to the right)

Triple-click anywhere in the paragraph.

```
F8, F8, F8, F8
```

> **TIP**   Selecting multiple paragraphs partially off the screen can be tedious with the mouse when the displayed portion shifts around erratically. To select multiple paragraphs precisely with the keyboard, use multiple `[F8]` to select the first paragraph, then `[Shift]` + `[Ctrl]` + `[Down Arrow]` until the highlight extends to the end of the last desired paragraph.

Selecting a section

```
F8, F8, F8, F8, F8
```

Selecting all text

AR: Click **Home** | **Select** (Editing group) | **Select All**.
BR/MAC: Click **Edit** | **Select All**.

```
F8, F8, F8, F8, F8, F8
```

```
Ctrl + A (MAC: Cmd + A)
```

Holding `[Shift]` while pressing `[F8]` will reduce the selection in the reverse order of the sequence above.

> **MAC** The Office use of `[F8]` conflicts with a default Mac OS X key assignment. To turn off the Mac OS use, click **Apple** | **System Preferences** | **Keyboard** (**Hardware** group). On the **Keyboard Shortcuts** tab clear the **On** check box for the key assignment.
>
> **MAC** The Office use of `[Shift]` + `[F8]` conflicts with a default Mac OS X Exposé key assignment. To turn off the Exposé use, click **Apple** | **System Preferences** | **Exposé** (**Personal** group) | **Spaces**. Under **Keyboard and Mouse Shortcuts,** on the pop-up menu for the shortcut, click —.

The Microsoft Word help lists ways to select more specialized objects such as parts of tables or rectangles of text.
Of course, rather than learning these special keys, you can simply rely on cursor movements. For example, to select the current line of text, move to its beginning with `[Home]` then extend the selection to the end of the line with `[SHIFT]` + `[END]`.

1.5.   Editing

Even if we hate to admit it, writers spend more time editing than writing. In ancient times they had to resort to whiteout and scissors to change a manuscript, methods that severely damage computer screens. Microsoft Word instead provides many functions to make rearranging text much easier—confusingly many functions. In the dark ages of the operating system schism, the microwizards and applites disagreed over how to do things. As a result, duplicate ways of performing common tasks exist in Word to this day. The following table lists the keystrokes for basic editing functions.

Table 1-5: Basic editing keys

`Ctrl + C` or `Ctrl + Insert`	Copy the selected text or object.
`Ctrl + Shift + C`	Copy formatting only (Format Painter).
`Ctrl + X` or `Shift + Delete`	Cut the selected text or object.
`Ctrl + V` or `Shift + Insert`	Paste current content of clipboard.
`Ctrl + Alt + V` (MAC `Ctrl + Cmd + V`)	Paste special (allows selecting format to paste).
`Ctrl + Shift + V`	Paste formatting only (Format Painter).
`Ctrl + Spacebar`	Remove formatting.
`Ctrl + Z` or `Alt + Backspace`	Undo an action.
`Ctrl + Y`	Redo or repeat an action.

MAC Many **Word for Windows** shortcuts work on the Macintosh, if you use the Command key ⌘ or `[Cmd]` instead of the Control key `[Ctrl]`, and the `[Option]` key instead of the Alternate key `[Alt]`. For example, to undo use `[Cmd] + [Z]`.

The clipboard allows quick duplication or moving of text through copy, cut, and paste. Word has augmented its power with the **Format Painter** ✄, a clipboard that applies only the formatting of a piece of text to another one. Conversely, if you only want the text without formatting, **Paste Special** allows pasting the clipboard content in a variety of formats, including unformatted.

Copying or cutting an object to the clipboard

Select the object then
AR: Click **Home | Copy/Cut** (**Clipboard** group).
BR: Click **Edit | Copy/Cut**.

Right-click the highlight and select **Copy/Cut**

`Ctrl + C` or `Ctrl + Insert`/`Ctrl + X` or `Shift + Delete`

Pasting text from clipboard *with* formatting

AR: Click **Home | Paste button** (**Clipboard** group).
BR: Click **Edit | Paste**.

Right-click the location and select **Paste**

`Ctrl + V` or `Shift + Insert`

Pasting text from clipboard *without* formatting

AR: Click **Home | Paste** *down triangle* ▾ (**Clipboard** group) | **Paste Special**.
BR: Click **Edit | Paste Special**.

```
Ctrl + Alt + V (MAC Ctrl + Cmd + V)
```

Copying formatting

Select the text with the correct formatting then
AR: Click **Home | Format Painter** (**Clipboard** group) or right-click text and select the paintbrush 🖌 from the formatting toolbar.
BR: Click the **Format Painter** button 🖌 on the **Formatting** toolbar.
Select the text to apply the formatting to.

> **TIP**   To apply the formatting to multiple locations **double-click** the **Format Painter** button 🖌.
> You can then highlight text with the brush cursor until you press [Esc].

Copying formatting to clipboard

Select the text with the correct formatting.

```
Ctrl + Shift + C (MAC Cmd + Shift + C)
```

> **TIP**   Use of the **Format Painter** button 🖌 also stores the format in the clipboard.

Applying formatting from clipboard

```
Ctrl + Shift + V (MAC Cmd + Shift + V)
```

Particularly when copying and pasting from web pages, you may accidentally insert new fonts and formatting in your document. Although the **Paste Special** function allows you to paste the text unformatted, it requires you to change the formatting every time you use it. When copying many passages of formatted text, a quick way to insert unformatted is desirable. Word does not provide a **Paste Unformatted** button or keyboard shortcut. To roll your own, copy the following code to the macro sheet for all documents and assign it to a keyboard shortcut, such as [Alt] + [Insert].

Creating a Paste Unformatted macro

Open the Microsoft Visual Basic editor as follows.
AR: Click **View | Macros** (**Macros** group).
BR/MAC: Click **Tools | Macro | Macros**.
Select a specific document or **All active templates and documents** from the **Macros in** list depending on whether you want the function available in one or all documents.
Enter a name into **Macro name**, for example "PasteUnformatted."
Click [Create]
In the code sheet enter the following text between the **Sub** and **End Sub** line. Do not remove any code created by Word.

```
Selection.PasteSpecial Link:=False, DataType:=20, Placement:=wdInLine,
    DisplayAsIcon:=False
```

Close the editor to save the code.
Run the macro as follows.
AR: Click **View | Macros** (**Macros** group).
BR: Click **Tools | Macro | Macros**.
Select the macro name from the list, for example "PasteUnformatted."

Click [Run]

Assigning a macro to a keyboard shortcut

AR: Click **File | Options | Customize Ribbon**, then next to Keyboard shortcuts [Customize].
O07: Click **Office | Word Options | Customize**, then next to Keyboard shortcuts [Customize].
BR: Click **Tools | Customize | Commands**, then [Keyboard].
MAC: Click **Tools | Customize | Customize Keyboard**.
In the **Customize Keyboard** dialog box select **Macros** from the **Categories** list.
Select the macro name from the **Macros** list, for example "PasteUnformatted."
Click in the **Press new shortcut key** field.
Press the desired keyboard shortcut combination, for example [Alt] + [Insert].
If the combination is already in use, Word displays **Currently assigned to** followed by the function name. If you want to use a different keystroke combination, erase the entry in the **Press new shortcut key** field and enter a different one.
Click [Assign]

AR: Assigning a macro to the Quick Access Toolbar

Click the *down triangle* ▼ at the right of the Quick Access Toolbar.
Click **More Commands**.
In the **Word Options** dialog box select **Macros** from the **Choose commands from** list.
Select a macro name like "Normal.NewMacros.PasteUnformatted" from the list below.
Click [Add > >]
Click [OK]

MAC: Assigning a macro to the Standard Toolbar

Right-click or control-click at the end of the **Standard Toolbar**.
Select **Customize Toolbars and Menus**.
In the **Customize Toolbars and Menus** dialog box select **Commands**, then **Macros** from the **Categories** list.
Click a macro name like "Normal.NewMacros.PasteUnformatted" in the Commands list and drag it to the place in the toolbar where you want the button to appear.
Click [OK] to close the dialog box.

Microsoft Word also has a number of tools to move disjointed parts of text quickly. First, you can select multiple passages of text by holding down the [Ctrl] (**MAC** [Cmd]) key while selecting text. Multiple highlighted passages are copied as one long piece of text, because the regular clipboard only stores one entry. The **Office Clipboard** stores twenty-four. Once activated, the usual copy and cut functions add entries to the Office Clipboard. The regular function pastes the last entry, the one at the top, as shown in Figure 1-11. Clicking any entry in the Office clipboard pastes it at the current cursor location.

MAC Word for Mac 2011 uses the Scrapbook instead of the Office Clipboard. Use [Ctrl] + [Cmd] + [C] to copy objects to the Scrapbook or open it with **View | Scrapbook** and click the **Add** button. You can also drag objects between the document and the Scrapbook window with the mouse. In prior versions of Word for Mac a more limited Scrapbook is accessible through the **Toolbox** button of the **Standard Toolbar** and **Tools | Scrapbook**.

Figure 1-11: Office Clipboard with four entries and Mac Scrapbook

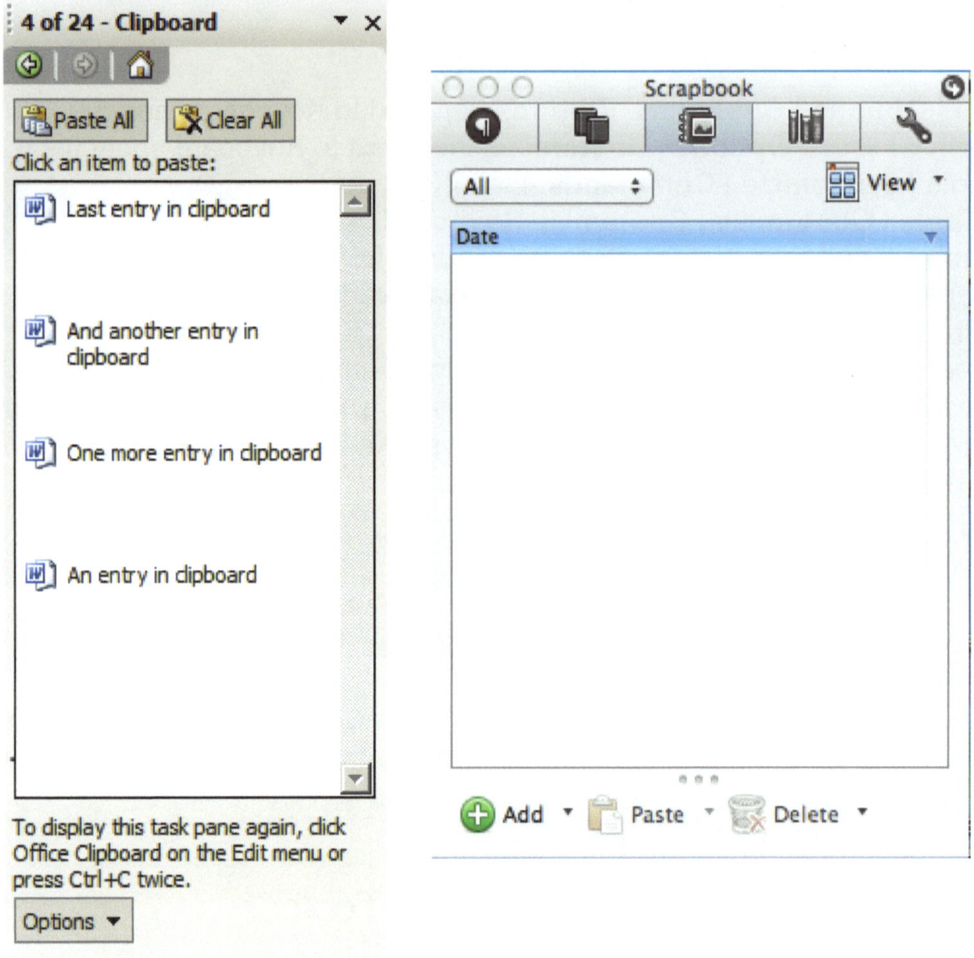

Open Office Clipboard

AR: Click **Home** | *Clipboard dialog launcher* ⬐ (the tiny arrow in the bottom right corner of the **Clipboard** group).
BR: Click **Edit | Office Clipboard**.

Select object

```
Ctrl + C, Ctrl + C
```

Word has a special storage location named the Spike for aggregating multiple disjointed items and quickly *moving* them to a single location with one paste operation. You can only cut items with [CTRL] + [F3]. Unlike the Office Clipboard, the removed text is *appended* to the existing content of the Spike. [CTRL] + [Shift] + [F3] inserts the entire content in a new location *and empties* the Spike.

Table 1-6: Special Clipboard keys

Ctrl + F3 (**MAC** Cmd + F3)	Cut to the Spike.
Ctrl + Shift + F3 (**MAC** Cmd + Shift + F3)	Paste and empty Spike.
Ctrl + C, Ctrl + C	Copy to Office Clipboard
MAC: Ctrl + Cmd + C	Copy to Mac Scrapbook

> **TIP**   If you want to use the Spike with the mouse, add the **Add to Spike** button to the Quick Access Toolbar. Click the *down triangle* ⩡ at the right of the QAT, then click **More Commands**. In **Choose commands from** select **Commands Not in the Ribbon**, then select **Spike** from the alphabetical list.
>
> **TIP**   You *cannot* undo the emptying of the Spike, but you can successively undo the moving of text to the Spike, thus restoring the cut items to their original location.

When filled, the Spike stores its content as AutoText (see 3.5). Inserting it as AutoText does *not* empty the Spike, thus allowing you to paste it multiple times.

Pasting content without emptying Spike

AR: Click **Insert | Quick Parts** (**Text** group) | **Building Blocks Organizer**.
BR/**MAC**: Click **Insert | AutoText | AutoText**.
Select **Spike** from the **Enter AutoText entries here** or **Building blocks** list.
The Spike entry only appears in the list after the Spike is filled.

The selection functions detailed in 1.4 allow precise selection of the text to manipulate. Word also provides shortcuts to deal with blocks of text. The following table lists some of them.

Table 1-7: Special editing keys (Windows)

Ctrl + Backspace	Delete one word to the left.
Ctrl + Delete	Delete one word to the right.
Alt + Shift + Down Arrow	Move selected paragraphs down.
Alt + Shift + Up Arrow	Move selected paragraphs up.
F2	Move selection to new location.
Shift + F2 ([Return] to paste)	Copy selection to new location.
Alt + Shift + R	Copy the header/ footer from previous section

Table 1-8: Special editing keys (Mac)

Fn + Delete or Delete⌦	Delete one character to the right.
Cmd + Delete	Delete one word to the left.
Cmd + Fn + Delete or Cmd + Delete⌦ or Cmd + Clear	Delete one word to the right.
Control + Shift + Down Arrow	Move selected paragraphs down.
Control + Shift + Up Arrow	Move selected paragraphs up.
F2	Cut selection.
F3	Copy selection.
F4	Paste selection.
Shift + F2 ([Return] to paste)	Copy selection to new location.
Control + Option + V	Copy from scrapbook.

Word does not provide a built-in function to cut a subclause ending in a comma, nor one for cutting the rest of the sentence before the period. To roll your own, copy the following code to the macro sheet for all documents and assign it to a keyboard shortcuts, such as [Ctrl] + [,]. Replace the comma in the code with a period or any other character as desired.

Creating a Cut To macro

Open the Microsoft Visual Basic editor as follows.
AR: Click **View | Macros** (**Macros** group).
BR/MAC: Click **Tools | Macro | Macros**.
Select a specific document or **All active templates and documents** from the **Macros in** list depending on whether you want the function available in one or all documents.
Enter a name into **Macro name**, for example "DeleteToComma."
Click [Create]
In the code sheet enter the following text between the **Sub** and **End Sub** line. Do not remove any code created by Word.

```
With Selection
.Extend Character:=","
.MoveLeft Unit:=wdCharacter, Count:=1, Extend:=wdExtend
End With
Selection.Cut
```

Close the editor to save the code.
Run the macro as follows.
AR: Click **View | Macros** (**Macros** group).
BR/MAC: Click **Tools | Macro | Macros**.
Select the macro name from the list, for example "DeleteToComma."
Click [Run]

See above for instructions on assigning a macro to a keyboard shortcut, the Quick Access Toolbar, or the Standard Toolbar.
With Word 2010's **Navigation Pane**, you can easily reorganize your documents by dragging and dropping headings and the following chapter instead of cutting and pasting them.

1.6. Find and Replace

Possibly the strongest advantage of computer files over paper documents is the ability to find something quickly. Microsoft Word takes the concept to incredible lengths with its many **Find** and **Go To** features. The following table lists the keystrokes to invoke the different functions. You can get by with remembering one keyboard shortcut, since Word combines most of the commands into the **Navigation Pane** or the **Find and Replace** window with multiple tabs, shown in Figure 1-12.

MAC In Word for Mac 2011 the Search Box on the right allows quick searching of the document. To get to the options in Figure 1-12 click the **Settings** Gear icon ⚙▾ in the **Find and Replace pane** on the left and select **Advanced Find & Replace**, then click the *down triangle* ▾ .

O13   In Word 2013 the **Navigation Pane** on the left allows quick searching and highlighting of phrases, but some functions are only available through the options in Figure 1-12. To get to them click the *down arrow* ▾ next to the **Find** field and select **Advanced Find**.

Since the Find and Replace window is independent of the main Word window, you can switch between editing and searching at will by clicking on one or the other. If you have a big enough screen, you can move the Find window to the side. When repeating the search the window floating above the text may obscure the context. The keyboard shortcuts [Shift] + [F4] or

[Alt] + [Ctrl] + [Y] (MAC [Cmd] + [G]) allow you to repeat the find with the window closed.

Table 1-9: Special movement keys (Windows)

Ctrl + F	Open Find window or Navigation task pane.
Ctrl + H	Open Replace window.
Ctrl + G or F5	Open Go To window.
Shift + F4 or Alt + Ctrl + Y	Repeat last Find or Go To after closing window.
Shift + F5 or Alt + Ctrl + Z	Move to previous edits.
Alt + Shift + F1 or Shift + F11	Go to the previous field.
Alt + F1	Go to the next field.
Alt + F7	Find the next misspelling or grammatical error.
Alt + Ctrl + Home	Open browse options list
Ctrl + PgDn	Move to the next browse object.
Ctrl + PgUp	Move to the previous browse object.

Table 1-10: Special movement keys (Mac)

Cmd + F	Open Find window or Navigation task pane.
Shift + Cmd + H	Open Replace window.
F5 or Option + Cmd + G	Open Go To window.
Shift + F4 or Cmd + G	Repeat last Find or Go To after closing window.
Shift + F5	Move to previous edits.
Shift + F11	Go to the previous field.
F11	Go to the next field.
Option + F7	Find the next misspelling or grammatical error.

1.6.1. Find and Replace

By default the Find and Replace window comes up in a simplified view without many options. Type in the text to find and hit [Find Next] to search for it. Word highlights the next occurrence of that phrase and changes the view as necessary to show it. Clicking [Find Next] again or using the keyboard shortcuts moves the highlight to the next occurrence. You can instead tell Word to highlight every occurrence of the find phrase instead, a useful function for getting a quick overview of repeated text in a section.

Highlighting all occurrences of a phrase

Open the **Find** window and enter the phrase in **Find what**.
AR: Under **Reading Highlight** select **Highlight All**.
BR: Check **Highlight all items found in** and click [Find All].

Clearing highlights of all occurrences of a phrase

AR: Open the **Find** window and under **Reading Highlight** select **Clear Highlight**.
BR: Click anywhere in the text.

TIP   If you highlight *one* word before invoking the **Find and Replace window**, Word automatically inserts it into the **Find what box**.

Figure 1-12: Find window with additional search options

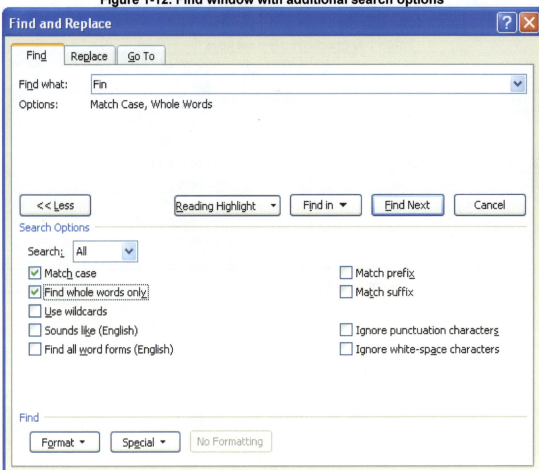

TIP   Word stores a list of the text and formatting of the last seven searches. To repeat a previous **Find** click the *down triangle* ☑ on the right of **Find what** and select an entry. Options are *not* stored with the list, so you have to select these again, if needed. **O13**: The **Navigation Pane** does not keep a search history.

Word allows more powerful searches by opening the options panel with the [More] button. A set of check boxes and special buttons become available as show in Figure 1-12.

O13   To set these options for the **Navigation Pane** click the *down triangle* ▾ , then **Options**.

Match case restricts the search to only words matching the case you enter. This comes in handy when looking for a name or an acronym. For example, if you have a character named "Fin," entering the correct case and checking Match case will skip any lower case versions of the word.

Find whole words only restricts the search to only words matching the text exactly with no additional letters. This is different from searching for the word followed by a space, since Microsoft Word also finds occurrences followed by punctuation marks such as commas and periods. Particularly when replacing words with only a few characters checking this option ensures that you do not accidentally replace them within other, longer words.

Use wildcards permits specifying complex entries to perform searches for phrases containing certain letters using a language commonly called *regular expressions*. For example, "deci*" will find phrases starting with "deci," such as "decide" or "decision." While other find functions take care of many of the common searches, specialized situations require wildcards, so I will delve into them quickly.

Table 1-11: Find and Replace Wildcards

?	Any single character.
*	Any string of characters.
<	Find *following* string at the beginning of a word.
>	Find *preceding* string at the end of a word
[ ]	One of the characters specified between the brackets.
[-]	Any single character in the range specified between the brackets.
[a-z]	Any single lowercase letter.
[A-z]	Any single letter regardless of case.
[0-9]	Any single number.
[!]	Not the character or expression following the exclamation mark.
{n}	Exactly *n* occurrences of the previous character or expression.
{n,m}	From *n* to *m* occurrences of the previous character or expression.
( )	Group characters into a single expression.
****	Take literally the character following this escape character.
\\n	*n*th expression in parentheses (**Replace with** only).

Regular expressions came from stream editors, programs that could automatically rearrange text based on rules. They are a programming language that allows powerful find and replaces. For example, if you confused a first and middle name a few times, a search for "(Maria) (Cathrine)" and a replace with "\2 \1" will flip the two words. If you do not have the programming mentality to figure out the expressions, the search options will satisfy almost all your needs.

For instance, the poorly named **Match prefix** and **Match suffix** options added in **Word for Windows 2007** limit searches to words that contain the string at the beginning or end, respectively, equivalent to the wildcards "<" and ">." So "dress" as prefix matches "dress" and "dresser," whereas "dress" as suffix matches "dress" and "address."

Rather than figure out the regular expressions needed for fuzzy searches, writers can use the options **Sounds like** and **Find all word forms**. For instance, if you do not remember the exact spelling of a characters name, searching for **Sounds like** "Catherine" will also find the variants "Cathrine" and "Katherine." **Find all word forms** helps in searches for irregular verbs and other grammatical constructs that change a word form. Microsoft Word uses the built-in spelling and grammar checking tools to look for related forms. For instance, searching for "find" will produce "find," "finding," and "found" as results. If your editor tells you the text contains too much passive voice, searching for "is" jumps to occurrences of "are" and "was," too, so you can work on them. Combining this search with **Highlight All** gives you a quick overview of the use of this verb in the text.

The misleading **Ignore punctuation characters** and **Ignore whitespace characters** added in **Word for Windows 2007** handle special search cases. Word does *not* ignore punctuation marks or whitespace characters, such as spaces or tabs, that you include in the search. The first option handles different regional settings. For example, searching for "90000" with **Ignore punctuation characters** finds both "90.000" and "90,000" regardless of the number formatting set in Microsoft Windows. Entering "010212" will find the dates "01-02-12" or "01/02/12."

The whitespace option deals with typesetting issues. If you used both spaces and tabs to align numbers, searching for " 90" with **Ignore whitespace characters** will find the number ninety preceded by either a space or tab.

Some of the most powerful find options appear in three inconspicuous buttons at the bottom of the Find window. Clicking on the first two reveals their power in the form of long menus. The **Format button** allows searching *and* replacing particular formatting. For instance, if I want to find occurrences of **TIP** blocks in this book without finding the word "tip" within other text, I can select **Font** from the menu and specify **Bold**. Word then only finds the word "tip" in boldface. Searches for phrases in color, superscript, different languages or styles are all possible. Clicking on the **Replace with** box applies the formatting with the replacement. For example, all MAC sections have a green marker. I could change them all to red by applying the **Font color: Green** to the **Find what** and **Font color: Red** to **Replace with**.

> **TIP**   You can search for formatting *without* entering any text. If, for instance, you need to find all internal dialogue in *italics*, leave **Find what** blank, click [Format], select **Font**, then **Italic**.

Table 1-12: Special Find and Replace characters

^p or ^13	Paragraph mark.
^t or ^9	Tab character.
^nnn	ASCII character, where nnn is the ASCII character code.
^0nnn	ANSI character, where nnn is the decimal character code preceded by zero.
^unnnn	Unicode character, where nnnn is the decimal character code.
^+	Em dash (—), for example converted from "--".
^=	En dash (–), for example converted from " - ".
^^	Caret (^).
^l or ^11	Manual line break, for example entered in text with [Shift] + [Enter]
^n or ^14	Column break.
^m	Manual page break, for example entered in text with [Ctrl] + [Enter] (also finds section breaks when wildcards are on).
^12	Page or section break (**Find what** only).
^b	Section break.
^s	Nonbreaking space, for example entered in text with [Ctrl] + [Shift] + [Spacebar].
^-	Optional hyphen, for example entered in text with [Ctrl] + [Hyphen].
^g or ^1	Picture or graphic (inline only).
^?	Any single character (Same as **?** with wildcards on).
^#	Any single digit (Same as **[0-9]** with wildcards on).
^$	Any single letter (Same as **[A-z]** with wildcards on).
^f or ^2	Footnote mark.
^e	Endnote mark.
^d or ^19 or ^21	Field code (the curly braces inserted *by Word* when field codes are visible).
^a or ^5	Comment.
^w	White space (any combination of spaces and tab characters).
^c	Windows Clipboard contents (**Replace with box** only)
^&	Contents of the **Find what box** (**Replace with box** only)

The **Special button** allows searching by wildcards, but also for special characters that matter in typesetting. Microsoft Word represents the search terms with a *circumflex accent* (^), also called a *caret*, followed by *lowercase* letters or numbers. Although known as wildcards, too, these are Word internal representation that should *not* be used with **Use wildcards** checked, which turns on the regular expressions discussed above. With that one exception, you can use the **Special button** or type the character combinations and check all other options as desired. Some, like **Em Dash**, are obvious and save you from having to enter an actual em-dash. Others require an explanation. The Table 1-12 summarizes their meaning.

Most special Find entries are for otherwise difficult to enter items. A computer can display more characters than show on the keyboard. As discussed, different systems of coding, such as ASCII, ANSI, and Unicode assign numbers to every possible character. The keystrokes used in 1.2 or the Symbols table do not work with the Find and Replace window. Instead, enter the caret (^) followed by the decimal ASCII code, a zero and the decimal ANSI code, or a lowercase u and the hexadecimal Unicode to search or replace special characters.

Some of the frequently used ones, such as the paragraph mark symbolizing a carriage return (ASCII 13) or a tab (ASCII 9) have mnemonic alternatives like ^p and ^t. For example, ^^, ^094, ^0094, or ^u005E all allow searching for a caret.

A number of special characters search for objects without a keyboard equivalent, such as section breaks, footnote marks, or graphics. The combination ^g only searches for inline graphics, those embedded in the text. It does not find floating graphics in frames, since those are in a separate layer independent of the text.

Two special combinations make bulk reformatting easier. Say you wanted to change the font, color, and size of every occurrence of a phrase. Do so with one example, then copy it to the clipboard. Open the Find window and paste the text into **Find what** and enter ^c into the **Replace with box**. Word replaces the text with the content of the clipboard *including formatting*. Alternatively, enter the phrase in **Find what**, enter ^& for **Replace with** to use the same text after replace, then format it using the [Format] button.

> **TIP**   After Ribbon, the **Next Footnote button** in the **Footnotes** group of the **References** tab also allows jumping to the next footnote. To jump to the next endnote, drop the menu with the *down triangle* ▾ .

The special combination ^d lets you search for fields, such as updatable dates. You must display field codes before searching. To show or hide all field codes in the document, press [ALT] + [F9] (**MAC** [Option] + [F9]). Hidden fields, like index entries, also require displaying hidden text. Use the **Show/Hide** button ¶ as shown in 1.2.

> **TIP**   Keyboard shortcuts like [Alt] + [F1] (**MAC** [F11]) find fields without the need to turn the display of field codes on.

1.6.2. Go To

Figure 1-13: Go To pane of Find and Replace window

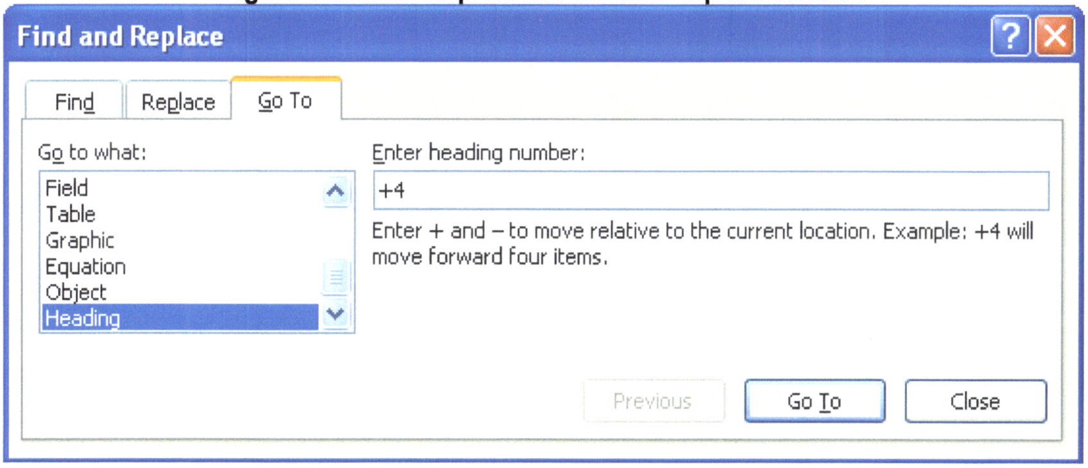

> **TIP**   **AR**: Clicking on the page or section number indicators in the **Status Bar** at the bottom of the Word screen opens the **Go To** window (**O13**: The page number opens the **Navigation Pane**).

The **Go To** pane of the **Find and Replace window** lets you move quickly among objects in the document. It accepts both absolute and relative entries. For example, to go to page 20, select **Page** in the **Go to what** list and enter "20" in the **Enter page number** box. Entering "+4" jumps forward four pages, whereas "-4" jumps back four pages. The same approach works when jumping among sections, lines, comments, footnotes, and endnotes, fields, tables, graphics, equations, objects, and headings. Bookmarks, however, require a specific selection from the list.

> **TIP**   If you use headings for chapter titles, as recommended, the **Go To** function lets you quickly jump to the beginning of a chapter by entering its heading number. You can also quickly move one chapter at a time with the **Browse** function described below by setting **Browse by Heading**.

1.6.3.   Browse

Word permits you to search for much more than text. The browse options list combines the functionality of the **Find and Replace window** with other commands to help you move among different objects. It is most useful for complex documents, like this book. When you hit [Alt] + [Ctrl] + [Home], Word presents a list of objects you can browse, including tables, headings, footnotes, and Find. Hovering with the cursor over a button displays its function in the title bar. The movement keys [Ctrl] + [PgDn] and [Ctrl] + [PgUp] then jump to the next or previous occurrence of that browse object. The keystroke combinations such as [Shift] + [F4] are special forms of the general browse functions, in this instance restricted to repeating the last **Find** or **Go To** action. Only [Alt] + [F7] for finding misspellings has no equivalent in the browse list.

> **O13**   The **Browse** buttons have disappeared. Use the **Navigation Pane** with the **Options** in the menu of the *down triangle* ▼ to search for graphics, tables, or comments. Unlike **Browse** the **Navigation Pane** *will* find floating images, those is a separate layer independent of text.

If the keystrokes do not work in your version of Word, the *browse arrows* and button below the vertical slider perform the same functions.

> **TIP**   Selecting **Browse by Edits** sets the *browse arrows* to move to the locations you last worked on like the keyboard shortcut [Shift] + [F5].

Some Word versions have a function to jump back to the last place you worked on when opening a document. To enable the jump automatically, create an **AutoOpen** macro. This special name tells Word to run the macro automatically when a document is opened. The keyboard shortcut [Shift] + [F5] is supposed to do this, too, but works unreliably.

Creating a macro to go back to the last location on open.

Open the Microsoft Visual Basic editor as follows.
AR: Click **View** | **Macros** (**Macros** group).
BR/**MAC**: Click **Tools** | **Macro** | **Macros**.

Select a specific document or **All active templates and documents** from the **Macros in** list depending on whether you want the function available in one or all documents.
If the name **AutoOpen** appears in the **Macro name** list, select it, and Click [Edit]. Otherwise enter "AutoOpen" into the field and Click [Create].
In the code sheet enter the following text between the **Sub** and **End Sub** line. Do not remove any code created by Word.

```
Application.GoBack
```

Close the editor to save the code.
The macro runs anytime you open a document.

Early **After Ribbon** versions did not properly store the last location on close. To simulate the behavior some users have resorted to setting a bookmark on save and jumping to it on open. The considerably more complex code is available on my web site www.WolfORourc.com and in the Microsoft Office forum on the web. The **AutoOpen** macro works again in **Office 2013**.

1.7.   Views

Word can display your document in different views. The **Normal View**, called **Draft** after Ribbon, maximizes the display by suppressing margins ands borders to show as much text as possible. By reducing page and section breaks down to place holders you can also quickly see and delete them. **Print Layout View**, called **Page Layout** in some versions, shows the document the way it looks when printed to paper, the preferred way when placing graphical elements and working with headers and footers. **Web Layout View**, called **Online Layout** in some versions, formats the pages the way they would look when published as a web page, without any breaks. **Outline View** allows you to collapse the text down to headings to quickly navigate through or move entire chapters. To facilitate quickly changing among views, Word always displays the **View Changer** at the bottom of the screen.

Figure 1-14: Word 2010 View Changer

Changing the document view.

AR: Click **View**, then the desired view in the **Document Views** group.
BR/**MAC**: Click **View**, then select the desired view or **Full Screen** from the menu.

Click on the desired view button in the View Changer at the bottom of the screen.

Alt + Ctrl + N (**MAC** Option + Cmd + N) (Switch to **Normal View**)
Alt + Ctrl + P (**MAC** Option + Cmd + P) (Switch to **Print Layout View**)
Alt + Ctrl + O (**MAC** Option + Cmd + O) (Switch to **Outline View**)

Full Screen Reading enters a special mode with minimal menus and toolbars to dedicate as much of the screen to reading as possible. Under **View Options** you can select to display one or two pages at once, increase the font size, and select other options to improve readability. Word turns off editing in this mode, so you don't have to worry about accidentally changing the document. You can allow typing under **View Options**. Before Ribbon Word split the function of this view into the **Reading Layout** and the **Full Screen** mode.

Exiting Full Screen, Reading Layout, or Read Mode view.

Select a different view from the menu, Ribbon, or **View Changer**.

Click the [Close] button on screen.

```
Esc
```

> **TIP**   To access the menu in **Full Screen** mode, move the cursor to the top of the screen until the menu bar appears.

Occasionally you may want to compare the same part in different views, or see two parts next to each other. Word allows you to split the screen horizontally, then navigate the two window panes independently.

Split the screen.

AR: Click **View | Split** (**Windows** group).
BR/MAC: Click **Windows | Split**.

Pull down the divider above the vertical scroll bar.

```
Alt + Ctrl + S (MAC Option + Cmd + S)
```
Move the split bar to where you want it.

Remove the split.

AR: Click **View | Remove Split** (**Windows** group).
BR/MAC: Click **Windows | Remove Split**.

Pull the split bar to the top.

Double-click the split bar.

```
Alt + Ctrl + S (MAC Option + Cmd + S)
```

```
Alt + Shift + S
```

> **TIP**   If you keep your research at the end of the document, splitting the screen allows you to view that material in one window pane, while continuing to write in the other.

2. Styles

Even if you do not write for a fashion magazine, you want to know about Word styles, sets of formatting that you can apply to text to change its appearance quickly. Microsoft considers styles so important that in the **Office Fluent** interface they devoted a good part of the **Home** Ribbon to the **Styles** gallery. Beyond formatting, Word uses styles for document organization and navigation, for example in **Outline View** discussed in 1.7. Self-publishing has raised their importance further. Whereas publisher may employ specialists to lay out a book, publishing web sites rely on the writer to format a document in a way that a program can automatically convert into a print-on-demand book or ebook without human intervention. Styles feature prominently in a successful conversion.

2.1. *Default Styles*

Templates govern the starting formatting of a new blank document. Out of the box, Word uses the Normal.dot template. A self-publishing service may provide other templates on their web site to ensure consistent formatting for their programs. Invariably these templates contain the definitions for a number of styles. You can simply apply them to your text without fiddling around with formatting. If you used the default styles, particularly **Normal** and the **Heading** styles, your text will automatically adjust, if you paste it into a publisher's template.

> **TIP**   To see a powerful demonstration of templates, click the **Change Styles** button at the right of the gallery, click **Style Set**, then hover over an entry. The screen updates to show the text in that style.

To get to the styles gallery, you have to navigate to the appropriate tab of the Ribbon at the top of the screen. When applying styles frequently, you can have a floating list of them within easier reach by opening the **Apply Styles** or **Styles** task panes, the narrow windows within Word that give access to the styles list. To anchor a task pane to the side, drag it past the edge of the Word window until it docks. To float it over the window again, drag it toward the middle until it undocks.

Opening the Styles/Apply Styles task pane.

AR: Click **Home**, then the **More** *down triangle* ▼ at the end of the gallery (**Styles** group), then select **Apply Styles** or click the *Styles dialog launcher* ⌐ (the tiny arrow in the bottom right corner of the **Styles** group).
BR: Click **Format | Styles and Formatting**.
MAC: Click **Format | Style** or **Home**, then the **Manage the style** button (**Styles** group).

```
Alt + O, S
```

```
Ctrl + Shift + S or Alt + Ctrl + Shift + S

(MAC Cmd + Shift + S)
```

The **Styles** task pane shows a list of styles, allowing quick application of many of them with one click, whereas the **Apply Styles** pane starts out with only one style visible, requiring you to open a drop-down menu. These correspond to the **Styles and Formatting** pane and **Styles** drop-down menu in the **Formatting** toolbar Before Ribbon. Hovering over an entry in the list of the **Styles** pane displays a description of the style's formatting. Either pane or the gallery highlight the style of the current paragraph, the one with the blinking cursor.

> **MAC** In Word for Mac 2011 the **Styles** task pane is the first tab of the Toolbox accessible through the Standard Toolbar (see Figure 1-5).
>
> **TIP   AR**: To get a preview of the styles in the **Styles** task pane as you see in the gallery, check **Show Preview** at the bottom of the pane.

To apply a style to a paragraph you merely select it from one of the lists. As listed in Table 2-1, you can also apply the most common default styles with keyboard shortcuts. If you want to change only a portion of the text, select it first, then apply the style. Some of them, particularly those for numbered or bulleted lists, can't be applied to individual characters. Word identifies them with a paragraph mark, a **pilcrow**, in the **Styles** pane. Others only change highlighted text and do not affect paragraph formatting like alignment or spacing. Word identifies these character styles with a lowercase **a** in the **Styles** pane. Styles that work with both paragraphs and characters are called linked type and identified in the pane with both an **a** and a **pilcrow**. This convention, however, started After Ribbon. Word 2003 identifies many styles as paragraph type, even though they format characters just the same. If in doubt, try them on highlighted text and see what happens. Tables and lists have their own styles to provide a consistent look to borders, shading, alignment, numbering, or bullets, the symbols placed before text.

2.1.1.   Normal

Everything is **Normal** until the writer or AutoFormat changes it. In a novel almost all the text will use this style. Setting up Normal governs the basic look and feel of the document. Most other styles inherit their basic properties from Normal. Self-publishing services have different requirements for the Normal style. Using it consistently ensures that you can quickly change your document to meet the requirements of various publications, thus giving your books the widest distribution possible. As of this writing, the self-publishing author has to use at least three different services to produce a print paperback, an ebook for Kindle, and ebooks for the other formats. Without styles, you may face hours of reformatting.

The Normal style specifies the font type and size of the body text, tab stops, and the alignment, indentation, and spacing of paragraphs. You should *never* format entire paragraphs individually without using a style. This idea is so important that I will repeat it for emphasis.

You should *never* format entire paragraphs individually without using a style.

For ease of reading, ebooks demand indents at the beginning of paragraphs, but no spacing between them. A print book may dispense with the indent, but have a blank line between paragraphs. If you used actual tab or space characters for the indent and blank lines for the spacing, you have to strip them out before sending the manuscript to an ebook service. If instead you defined the indentation and spacing in the Normal style, a few clicks suffice to change the look of the entire document.

Since every template contains a definition for the **Normal** style, text copied to a template will automatically adjust. Except for *words that you format individually, like this part in italics,* the text will appear in the font and size of the **Normal** style in the template. So instead of Arial in this document, it may change to Book Antiqua.

> **TIP**   Templates created in certain Word versions by default *copy* the styles of the source document during a paste. If you want to use the template's styles instead, *undo the paste* to remove the copied styles, click the *down triangle* ▼ under the **Paste** button and under **Paste Options** select **Use Destination Theme** or **Merge Formatting**.

Normal is the base style, the underlying style on which most other styles in a document are dependent. Changes made to it update other styles to match, unless specifically overwritten in their definition.

> **TIP** Modify **Normal** to suit your needs first, so you can override its properties when creating new styles. As the base style for most others, any changes you make to **Normal** later will reflect in all these other ones.

For fiction, consider defining the **Paragraph** property **Special** under **Indentation** to "First Line" **By** 0.3 inches. During the writing process, you may also want to change the **Line spacing** to "Double" to facilitate printing handouts for editing.

> **TIP** Since **Normal** has a type of "paragraph," you can apply the style to entire paragraphs, but not characters. If you want to revert a few words of text within a paragraph back to **Normal**, use the **Format Painter** described in 1.5.

For existing documents, you may face the issue that the text contains a mix of leading spaces and tabs that cause inconsistent displays and large indentations when you redefine the **Normal** style. Find and Replace with the special characters from Table 1-12 helps clean up such issues. As we discussed earlier, to the computer the file is a stream of characters, some of which provide Word the formatting information to display the text on screen. From its point of view, leading characters at the beginning of a paragraph actually follow a carriage return, which appears on screen as a paragraph mark. Figure 2-1 shows the setup to remove characters following paragraph marks.

Figure 2-1: Find and Replace setup for leading white space

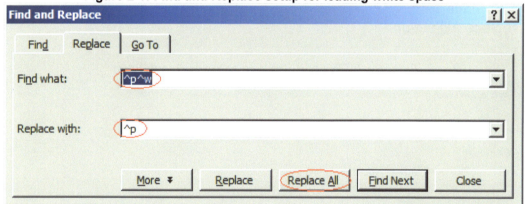

Searching for paragraph marks followed by space characters and replacing them with paragraph marks gets rid of leading spaces, allowing you to achieve consistent indentation by defining the paragraph style instead. If you do not use tabs in tables or in the middle of paragraphs, replacing all tabs with nothing will work the same, but the paragraph mark method is safer, just in case you overlooked some tab character with a special use. Certainly, replacing all space characters with nothing will leave your text a mess of black.

The controlled way calls for replacing leading tabs and spaces separately. As the text may contain multiple leading spaces, you may have to determine the different number of spaces used and run multiple replaces. Or, you keep hitting the [Replace All] button until Word reports zero replacements.

> **TIP** If you also used spaces or tabs to center text, search for ^p^t or ^p (space after the p) and convert all those lines to use the **Centered** or **Title** style (see 2.3) before you run the following find and replace.

Removing all leading tab characters

Open the **Find and Replace** window (see 1.6.1).
Enter ^p^t for **Find what**.
Enter ^p for **Replace with**.
Click the [Replace All] button until Word reports it has made "0 replacements."

Removing all leading space characters

Open the **Find and Replace** window (see 1.6.1).
Enter ^p for **Find what**. Note the space after the "^p."
Enter ^p for **Replace with**.
Click the [Replace All] button until Word reports it has made "0 replacements."

Replacing spaces and tabs individually may require multiple passes, as you may have mixed tabs and spaces. For non-fiction, such as this book, you may have lines that should contain leading spaces. In fiction, the indentation of the **Normal** style usually makes them unnecessary. You can take advantage of Word's special search characters "^w" to wipe out all white space after paragraph marks in one search.

Removing all leading tab and space characters

Open the **Find and Replace** window (see 1.6.1).
Enter ^p^w for **Find what**.
Enter ^p for **Replace with**.
Click the [Replace All] button.

Figure 2-2: Find and Replace setup for blank lines

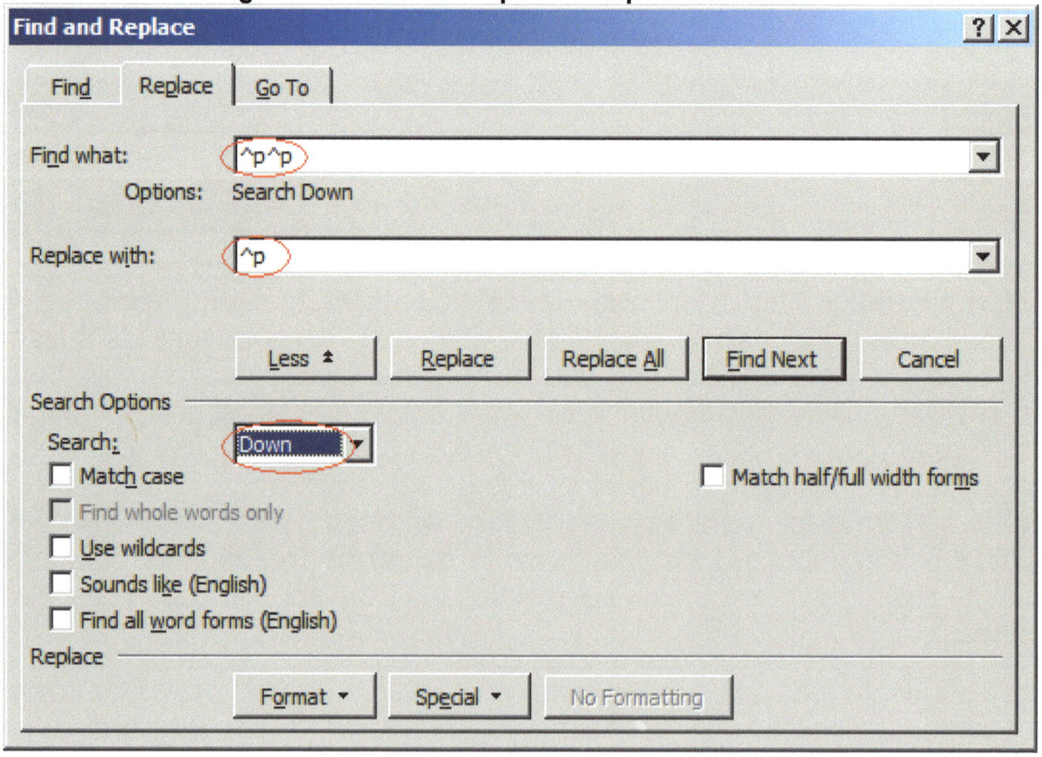

Similarly, if your text contains blank lines to separate paragraphs, you should remove them, so ebook readers can render the paragraphs as they need. For Word a blank line is merely a carriage return preceded by nothing other than another carriage return. To remove them from a text, look for two paragraph marks and replace them with one. Repeat the search until Word reports zero replacements. If you used blank lines for spacing in the preliminary materials, known as front matter, and you want to keep them, replace from the first chapter down. Figure 2-2 shows the setup.

Removing blank lines in body matter

Place the cursor at the beginning of the first chapter.
Open the **Find and Replace** window (see 1.6.1).
Enter ^p^p for **Find what**.
Enter ^p for **Replace with**.
Click [More] to open the **Search Options**, if needed.
Set the **Search** field to "Down," if needed.
Click the [Replace All] button.
If Word asks whether you want to continue searching from the beginning, click [No].
Repeatedly click the [Replace All] and [No] buttons until Word reports it has made "0 replacements."

2.1.2.   Heading *n*

For a writer the **Heading** styles rank second in importance. Heading styles usually make a single line stand out, such as chapter titles, and feature bold face type, larger font size, and, numbering. Whereas fiction will generally only use the top level **Heading 1**, non-fiction, like this book, can continue down the line with ever-finer subdivisions. As set up in many templates, higher heading numbers indent further and add additional numbering to subdivide the text visually. Do not confuse the *headings* with the *headers*, the text shown at the top of pages. Headers have their own style and do not organize the document in any way.

The benefits in Word alone justify using headings. As discussed in 1.6, the **Go To** and **Browse** function allow jumping from one heading to the next. You can tell Word to automatically build a table of contents (see 4.3) out of the headings, then control click an entry to jump to that chapter. The **Navigation Pane** introduced in Word 2010 also organizes the document by headings, and just like in **Outline View** (see 1.7), you can move entire chapters around quickly by dragging their headings.

Self-publishing has raised the stakes further for proper use of styles. Some ebook conversion programs use headings to identify chapters and force page breaks. Print-on-demand templates often include heading styles to ensure that they print correctly. Save yourself the trouble later and use headings to identify your chapters right from the start.

When using **Heading 1** as chapter title, consider modifying the style (see 2.2) to turn on **Numbering**, so the chapter number is automatically included and updated as you move chapters around. For the print version, you can check **Page break before** on the **Line and Page Breaks** tab of the **Paragraph** dialog box to ensure that each chapter starts on a new page. Clearing just this one box before sending the document for ebook conversion then removes *all* these page breaks, so the ebook reader can format the text continuously.

TIP   Some ebook conversion programs cannot handle the automatic heading numbering. You can still use the benefit of automatic renumbering during the document creation process and change the fields to text right before conversion (see 7.2.6).

2.2.   Style Basics

To apply the style to an entire paragraph, click anywhere within it to place the blinking cursor there. To apply the style only to certain characters, select the text using one of the methods discussed in 1.4.

Table 2-1: Styles related keys (Windows)

`Ctrl + Shift + N`	Apply **Normal** style.
`Ctrl + Alt + 1`	Apply **Heading 1** style.
`Ctrl + Alt + 2`	Apply **Heading 2** style.
`Ctrl + Alt + 3`	Apply **Heading 3** style.
`Ctrl + Shift + S`	Activate **Apply Style** pane.
`Alt + Ctrl + Shift + S`	Open **Styles** pane.

Table 2-2: Styles related keys (Mac)

`Cmd + Shift + N`	Apply **Normal** style.
`Cmd + Option + 1`	Apply **Heading 1** style.
`Cmd + Option + 2`	Apply **Heading 2** style.
`Cmd + Option + 3`	Apply **Heading 3** style.
`Cmd + Shift + S`	Activate **Apply Style** pane.

Applying a style

AR: Click **Home**, then select a style from the gallery (**Styles** group). If the desired style is not visible, use the *triangle* buttons on the right to expand the **Quick Style** list, a table of commonly used styles, or scroll through the gallery.

AR: In the **Apply Styles** task pane click the *down triangle* ▼ next to the **Style** field and select a style, or type the name of a style.
BR: In the **Formatting** toolbar click the *down triangle* next to the **Style** field and select a style.
MAC: In the **Standard** toolbar click the **Formatting Palette** button, then **Styles**.

In the **Styles** task pane click the desired style.

Use a keyboard shortcut from Table 2-1 to apply one of the default styles.

You can modify styles to suit your needs or create new ones. For example, if you want your chapter titles centered instead of left aligned, change **Heading 1** accordingly. Word opens up the same dialog boxes used by the various formatting choices, except you get to them through the styles tools.
The **Modify Style** dialog box, shown in Figure 2-3, has buttons for common formatting choices such as font, **bold**, *italic*, alignment, and spacing in the **Formatting** section.

Modify a style

Right-click a style entry in the gallery, **Quick Style** list, or **Styles** task pane, then select **Modify**.

Hover with the cursor over a style name in the **Styles** task pane. Click the down arrow that appears to its right, then select **Modify**.

In the **Apply Styles** pane click the [Modify] button.

To access additional formatting choices click the [Format] button to open a drop-down menu. The entries, such as "Font" or "Paragraph," open the same dialog boxes available through the respective dialog launchers in the Ribbon or the choices in the menu.

> **TIP** If you want to assign a keyboard shortcut to a frequently used style, modify it, click the [Format] button, then select **Shortcut key** from the menu.

Figure 2-3: Modify Style dialog box

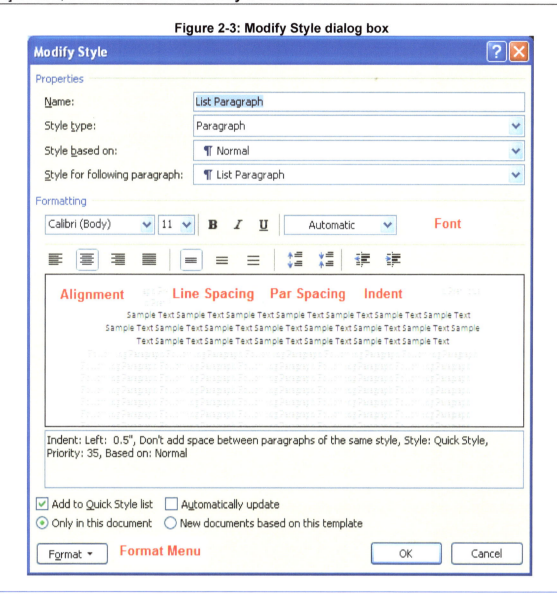

Turning on Numbering for Headings

To add automatically updating sequential number fields (see 4) to the beginning of every heading of a level, turn on **Numbering**.
Modify the appropriate **Heading** style as shown above.
Click [Format].
Click **Numbering** on the menu.
Select a numbering format in the **Numbering and Bullets** dialog box.
Click [OK].

You can also use the formatting commands you know on a text, or take an existing text, then convert it to a style.

Update a style to match text

Click anywhere in a paragraph with the right formatting to place the blinking cursor there. Right-click a style entry in the gallery or **Styles** task pane, then select **Update … to Match Selection**.

Create a style to match text

Click anywhere in a paragraph with the right formatting to place the blinking cursor there.
AR: Click the **More** *down triangle* ⏷ next to the gallery and select **Save Selection as a New Quick Style** (**O13**: **Create a style**).
BR: In the **Styles** task pane, click the [New Style] button.
Change the properties as needed.

Every style other than **Normal** is based on another style. When you change a formatting element of the base style, all styles that originate from it will also reflect the change. Consider this choice carefully when creating new styles. The closer the base style already matches the new one, the less unexpected consequences later.

> **TIP**   To make printouts for critiquing or submissions set the line spacing to double with the ≡ button in the **Modify Style** dialog box. For publication set it to single-spaced with ☰.

Every style also specifies a style for the following paragraph. In most instances select **Normal**. This setting means that Word will automatically revert to the Normal style, when you start a new paragraph. Occasionally you may want to continue in a different style, for example, if you defined one named Dialogue. To save you the trouble of applying the style again and again to every line of dialogue in an exchange, set the following style to Dialogue, too. Remember to switch back to **Normal** style when the narrative picks up again.
Some styles have the **Automatically update** box checked. Microsoft Word detects when you change the formatting of a paragraph and then automatically updates the style to match. Usually you do *not* want this to happen, as the update will cascade through all styles based on the changed one. Word sets this option by default for specialized styles such as **TOC**, used with table of contents (see 4.3), where directly applied formatting otherwise is lost when the table of content is updated.
Specialized styles such as **TOC**, **Index**, or those for tables usually do not display in the gallery or the **Styles** task pane. To modify them, change the options of the pane to display all styles, or use the **Manage Styles** dialog box which lists all styles in its lists, including those marked **Hide Until Used**.

Making all styles visible in the **Styles** task pane

AR: Click **Options** and change the **Select styles to show** drop-down list to **All styles**, or click the [Manage Styles] button at the bottom of the task pane to open the **Manage Styles** dialog box.
BR: Change **Show** at the bottom of the task pane to **All styles**, or set it to **Custom** to open the **Format Settings** dialog box, then click the [Style] button to open the **Styles** dialog box. Despite its label **All styles** does *not* show all styles. Those unchecked in **Format Settings** will not appear in the task pane, but do show up in the **Styles** dialog box.
MAC: Change **List** at the bottom of the task pane to **All styles**.

> **TIP** You can also modify the table of contents and index styles through the [Modify] buttons of their respective dialog boxes (see 4.3 and 4.4).

2.3. More Styles

Beyond the default styles a book usually needs a few others. First, you should create a **Centered** style based on **Normal** with a paragraph alignment of "centered" and *no indent* for the book title and scene break symbols. To avoid issues with later changes, consider using the built-in **Title** style for the preliminary materials and creating a separate **Centered** one for the body. If you prefer blank lines as scene breaks, create a new style **Before Break** from **Normal** where the **Paragraph** setting **Spacing** has **After** set to the height of the font, usually 12 or 10 pt, then apply the style to the paragraph preceding the break. If you want two blank lines, double the value. Since ebook devices may place the paragraph at the end of a page, making the break invisible, I recommend using symbols that cause no problems in Microsoft Word or publishing tools, such as three plus signs (+++), with a new style **Scene Break** that includes **Spacing** before and after.

Word includes separate styles **Header** and **Footer** to allow formatting of these page elements without affecting other parts of the book. Particularly when building anthologies with many sections (see 5.3) containing different headers, using styles ensures their formatting stays consistent.

> **TIP** To keep changes in sync with the **Header**, make it the base style for the **Footer**.

Many templates include two built-in styles to set apart quotes from the rest of the text. **Quote** uses the customary *italics* for one or two sentences. For larger passages, like newspaper clippings or broadcast segments, **Block Text** indents the information on both sides in addition and adds an accent color. You can redefine these to your own liking, of course.

> **TIP** `[Shift] + [F3]` (**AR**: Click **Home | Change Case** Aa ⌄ in the **Font** group) toggles the text between lower case, proper case with initial caps, and all upper case. Rather than using all upper case letters for quoted text, consider setting the **Font Effects** of the **Block Text** style to **All caps** instead. Should an ebook publisher demand it, you can convert those passages back to regular case with only a single change in style. The **Small caps** font improves readability by using larger letters for any capitalization in the text.

Non-fiction may require many more styles with intricate relationships. All key strokes in this book use a variant of the base style `Shortcuts` with a font of `Courier New`. Besides giving all keystrokes a consistent look, should I ever want to replace them with keyboard symbols, I can search the text for any occurrence of that style (see 1.6.1).

All the tip boxes use a style with a box around the paragraph. The detailed steps start with a style of **Heading 4** that adds a blue line as **Border** above the first paragraph. The built-in style also adds each task to the document outline, although that level is not included in the table of contents for now. The regular text picks up with a style named **Post H4**, a variant of **Normal** that merely adds the closing blue line.

Setting apart alternate approaches to the same task with dashed blue lines is more difficult. If two paragraphs have overlapping borders, Word either wipes them out or doubles them up, making a single, thicker line. Detailed steps using menus hence use variants of the **Normal** style with a dashed line above (Alternate End) or dashed lines above and below (Alternate Middle). Similarly, steps involving only keystrokes use variants with dashed lines of the style `Shortcuts` named `Shortcuts End` and `Shortcuts Middle`. By basing them on the created `Shortcuts` I ensure that their properties change, if I adjust the base style.

Word automatically uses an appropriate list or table style, when you create these objects. If you want to apply a custom one, base it on a style of the appropriate type to ensure that the special formatting of lists and tables are maintained. Similarly, table of contents and indexes created by Word have their own styles. Any objects with special properties deserve their own style to allow changing them independent of each other. All macrocode snippets in this book, for instance, uses a style named `Code`. All paragraphs containing figures use a **Figure** style to center them and ensure proper spacing, while the captions have the built-in style **Caption** with the paragraph option **Keep with next** set to prevent separation of the two objects.

> **TIP**   To make new styles available in other documents based on the same template, in the **Modify Style** dialog box select the **New documents based on this template** button (**AR**), or check **Add to template** (**BR**).

Word also includes two character styles, *Emphasis* and **Strong** that apply *italics* and **bold** to text. It may seem excessive to use a style for a few words. Different countries have different formatting guidelines. Using styles allows you to easily change to a different way to place emphasis, such as underline, to accommodate local customs. Particularly manuals and guides have need for character styles. This book distinguishes between **Word for Windows** and **Word for Mac** with two styles named "**WfW**" and "**WfM**" that apply different font colors.

3. Automatic Writing

How would you like to have Microsoft Word write the text for you? It's possible, but those wishing for a button that automagically finishes an entire novel, I have to disappoint you. Microsoft Word does not do that, yet. Parts of writing are repetitive, however. A number of functions, like Find and Replace, AutoCorrect, AutoFormat, and AutoText, can speed up your work.

3.1. Writing with Find and Replace

Some words occur frequently in a book, particularly names of people, objects, and places. Typing them over and over is time consuming and error prone, particularly foreign names with unusual spellings. In novels with many characters, embarrassing substitution of one name with another can happen. Using abbreviations offers consistency *and* speed.

Take for example a novel with the names in Table 3-1. Typing the abbreviation on the left allows you to later on perform a global find and replace (see 1.6) with the terms on the right. Special characters like the hash tag (#) ensure that letters within other words are not accidentally replaced. Obviously, if your work uses the hash tag for other purposes within the text, pick a different symbol to identify your favorite abbreviations. You can simplify your typing with seldom-used letters like "q" or "x" in conjunction with the **Find whole words only** option.

Table 3-1: Sample abbreviations for Find and Replace

#c	Cathrine
#l	Carlisle
#v	Calvin
#t	Tamalpais
#pt	President Tamalpais
xdc	Washington, DC
qbh	Beverly Hills
#pa	parallel
#mi	Mississippi
clt	couldn't
#bo	Bolívar
#rsa	Reproduction Services Administration
#fr	**Find and Replace window**
#ls	Lover, lover,^lYou are mine,^lNobody elses,^lYou are forever mine
#hr7	^&th Hussar Regiment

Replace can also deal with often-misspelled words, as the entries "#pa" and "#mi" show. Abbreviations like "clt" can replace cumbersome typing of "couldn't" with an apostrophe, or "#bo" substitutes for "Bolívar" with an accent over the i. To avoid surprises, check **Find whole words only** when replacing words without a special symbol. Using the power of the [Format] button in the **Find and Replace** window ensures consistent formatting, too, if for instance you want names of functions always displayed in bold, as is done in this book.

Take for example this segment, formatted as Block Text. Note particularly the use of the hash tag with #sis so the proper use of the abbreviation SIS is not replaced.

> "Mom! Mom! They'll kill me!" #v's screams made her blood curdle. "Mom, don't let them take me. Mom!"
> #c stood on the white front porch of her qbh house and looked at the ground. What cld she say? What cld she do? She had signed the agr 15 years ago. At 18. When she had no clue and no cares. Her failure to live up to it may doom her son now.
> A lieutenant of the qed handed her a writ of attachment and a rpt with the big letters "SIS" on top. "By order of the court of qla County one #v #l is hereby attached, in satisfaction of your contract with the #rsa, for failure to maintain the required #sis."
> The dreaded SIS, bane of every consort wannabe. Ratings given by girls that went on dates with him made up the most important part. To #c's amazement, #v had done poorly on his social outings, despite his pedigree. After all, his fa, famous Latin lover #r, was one of the most coveted #pos around. Tears rolled down her cheeks. Her small Maltese, #b, stood next to her and barked incessantly.

All names, including those of frequently used organizations, are done as abbreviations with hash tags. If you dislike using shift keys, prefixing q or x works the same, with the above caveat. Note also the use of abbreviations for commonly used longer words. Think of writing this way as using shorthand for the computer. Running find and replace one-by-one then substitutes the expansions to yield the following.

> "Mom! Mom! They'll kill me!" Calvin's screams made her blood curdle. "Mom, don't let them take me. Mom!"
> Cathrine stood on the white front porch of her Beverly Hills house and looked at the ground. What could she say? What could she do? She had signed the agreement 15 years ago. At 18. When she had no clue and no cares. Her failure to live up to it may doom her son now.
> A lieutenant of the Enforcement Department handed her a writ of attachment and a report with the big letters "SIS" on top. "By order of the court of Los Angeles County one Calvin Carlisle is hereby attached, in satisfaction of your contract with the Reproduction Services Administration, for failure to maintain the required Social Interaction Score."
> The dreaded SIS, bane of every consort wannabe. Ratings given by girls that went on dates with him made up the most important part. To Cathrine's amazement, Calvin had done poorly on his social outings, despite his pedigree. After all, his father, famous Latin lover Rodrigo, was one of the most coveted possessions around. Tears rolled down her cheeks. Her small Maltese, Buddy, stood next to her and barked incessantly.

In combination with the [Special] button, you can construct intricate text passages. For example, if your character regularly casts a love spell written in four lines, the replacement entry for #ls in the table above automatically inserts manual line breaks. If applied with a style like "Centered" during the replace, the spell will appear on four centered lines.

The entry #hr7 demonstrates how to minimize work with numbered items using a two-part replace.

First, enter #hr^# for **Find what** and ^&th Hussar Regiment for **Replace with**. The special combination ^# tells word to accept any single number after the #hr. The special combination "^&" is replaced with the text in **Find what**. The following results.

Any "#hr4" becomes "#hr4th Hussar Regiment."
Any "#hr5" becomes "#hr5th Hussar Regiment."
Any "#hr6" becomes "#hr6th Hussar Regiment."
Etc.

Now, find #hr and replace it with nothing, and with only two passes you can replace abbreviations for six regiments.

The find-and-replace method (FARM) of writing is a considerable time saver on larger pieces of text, but you do not discover incorrect abbreviations or unexpected replaces until a re-read. Set Word to only search from your current starting point down to not disturb already edited text. Retyping every find and every replace text and setting needed options becomes time consuming and tedious. Automating the task with macros minimizes the issues. The following code snippets handle common cases. The global template Normal.dot makes frequently used words like "could" available in all documents. By limiting story-specific, short abbreviations to a macro in the document, you can change them, as you work on different files. Detailed instructions for creating macros and assigning shortcut keys to them are in chapter 1.5.

FARM macro for general replace

The following code replaces "#cc" with "Cathrine Carlisle" in the entire document (.Wrap = wdFindContinue) and turns off all search options. The first two lines clear any formatting set with the [Format] button.

```
Selection.Find.ClearFormatting
Selection.Find.Replacement.ClearFormatting
With Selection.Find
   .Text = "#cc"
   .Replacement.Text = "Cathrine Carlisle"
   .Forward = True
   .Wrap = wdFindContinue
   .Format = False
   .MatchCase = False
   .MatchWholeWord = False
   .MatchByte = False
   .MatchWildcards = False
   .MatchSoundsLike = False
   .MatchAllWordForms = False
End With
Selection.Find.Execute Replace:=wdReplaceAll
```

Word remembers the search options in following replaces. If you group words with the same options together, following code can be reduced to five lines.

```
With Selection.Find
   .Text = "#dp"
   .Replacement.Text = "Deborah Perry"
End With
Selection.Find.Execute Replace:=wdReplaceAll
```

FARM macro for whole-word replace

To replace whole words only, set .MatchWholeWord = True as shown in the following code.

```
With Selection.Find
    .Text = "cld"
    .Replacement.Text = "could"
    .Forward = True
    .Wrap = wdFindContinue
    .Format = False
    .MatchWholeWord = True
    .MatchByte = False
    .MatchWildcards = False
    .MatchSoundsLike = False
    .MatchAllWordForms = False
End With
Selection.Find.Execute Replace:=wdReplaceAll
```

FARM macro for replace down

To avoid disturbing already edited text above, place the cursor at the beginning of the new section and set the options to search down (.Forward = True) and stop at the end (.Wrap = WdFindStop).

```
With Selection.Find
    .Text = "xdc"
    .Replacement.Text = "Washington, DC"
    .Forward = True
    .Wrap = WdFindStop
    .Format = False
    .MatchWholeWord = True
    .MatchByte = False
    .MatchWildcards = False
    .MatchSoundsLike = False
    .MatchAllWordForms = False
End With
Selection.Find.Execute Replace:=wdReplaceAll
```

FARM works best for temporary jobs, like minor characters that only occur frequently in one or two scenes in one document. There are better methods for shortcuts that you may use for months or years across multiple works.

3.2. Keyboard Shortcuts

Microsoft Word has many keyboard shortcuts for frequently used symbols. The following table lists some of those used by writers. The **Symbol** dialog box (see 1.2) shows defined hot key combinations for more items. Word also lets you roll your own by assigning keystrokes to many other characters.

Table 3-2: Keyboard shortcuts for common symbols

Symbol	Windows Shortcut	MAC Shortcut
— (em dash)	Alt + Ctrl + Minus Sign	Cmd + Option + Minus Sign
© (copyright)	Alt + Ctrl + C	Option + G
… (ellipsis)	Alt + Ctrl + Period	Option + ; (semicolon)
' (open quote)	Ctrl + `, `	Option +]
' (close quote)	Ctrl + ', '	Option + Shift +]
" (double quote)	Ctrl + `, "	Option + [
" (double close)	Ctrl + ', "	Option + Shift + [
¢ (cent)	Ctrl + /, C	Option + 4
° (degree)	Ctrl + @, Space	Option + Shift + 8
à (A grave)	Ctrl + `, A	Option + `, A
á (A acute)	Ctrl + ', A	Option + E, A
è (E grave)	Ctrl + `, E	Option + `, E
é (E acute)	Ctrl + ', E	Option + E, E

Assigning a keyboard shortcut to a symbol

Open the **Symbol** dialog box (see 1.2)
Click the symbol in the table.
Click [Shortcut Key] or [Keyboard Shortcut].

AR: Click **File | Options | Customize Ribbon**, then next to Keyboard shortcuts [Customize].
O07: Click **Office | Word Options | Customize**, then next to Keyboard shortcuts [Customize].
BR: Click **Tools | Customize | Commands**, then [Keyboard].
MAC: Click **Tools | Customize | Customize Keyboard**.
In the **Customize Keyboard** dialog box select **Common Symbols** from the **Categories** list.
Select the symbol from the **Common Symbols** list.

In the **Customize Keyboard** dialog box click in the **Press new shortcut key** field.
Press the desired keyboard shortcut combination.
If the combination is already in use, Word displays **Currently assigned to** followed by the function name. If you want to use a different keystroke combination, erase the entry in the **Press new shortcut key** field and enter a different one.
Click [Assign]

These keyboard shortcuts may save you some time compared to using the **Symbol** dialog box, if you remember them. Some of the combinations pose challenges. The em dash requires a minus sign key on the numeric keypad, not the hyphen. Often other programs or the operating system may intercept a keystroke sequence, leading to unexpected results. Instead of going through all the trouble for one character, Word lets you substitute words or phrases with other means.

3.3. *AutoCorrect/AutoFormat*

Word comes with functions to replace what you type with what it thinks you meant to type. Some people abhor this Word-does-what-it-wants-to-do-voodoo, but in the capable hands of a Word wizard, AutoCorrect and AutoFormat become powerful tools. While fundamentally distinct commands, even Word treats them as closely related by grouping their options in one dialog box. For the users the effects are indistinguishable. Something magically changes what they type, whether they like it or not.

As the name implies, AutoCorrect fixes typing mistakes. Word changes common typos like "yuo" to "you." It capitalizes first letters after a period, or adds expected punctuation marks, such as changing "im" to "I'm." AutoCorrect even recognizes common ways to type symbols and replaces them, such as changing "(c)" to "©." Following this book's convention, the commas in Table 3-3 mean press and release the key, where [Character] is any alphanumeric key.

Table 3-3: Auto shortcuts for common symbols

Symbol	Shortcut
— (em dash)	[Character], Hyphen, Hyphen, [Character]
© (copyright)	(, C,)
… (ellipsis)	., ., . (period)
' (open quote)	', [Character]
' (close quote)	[Character], '
" (double quote)	", [Character]
" (double close)	[Character], "
☺ (smiley)	:,)
→ (arrow)	Hyphen, Hyphen, >

AutoFormat, by contrast, deals with formatting issues and some punctuation. If Word recognizes you typing a numbered or bulleted list starting with *, -, or > followed by a space, it converts all the lines in the list to the appropriate Word styles. Two hyphens surrounded by characters turn into an em dash. Ordinal numbers like "12th" are forced to superscript "12th," and common fractions like "1/2" are replaced with the matching fraction character, for example "½ ." Internet addresses become hyperlinks. Leading spaces turn into tabs. Finally, when using Word as editor in the Outlook e-mail program, AutoFormat also recognizes the old-style way to indicate formatting in e-mail such as "*bold*" and "_italic_" and replaces it with the real formatting.

For most parts, AutoCorrect replacements trigger on a word boundary, i.e. when you type a space or punctuation mark, but replacement of symbols happens the moment Word recognizes them. AutoFormat, by contrast, needs to recognize what you are doing in context. For example, replacement of an em-dash only triggers if the two hyphens are followed by letters or quotes without intervening spaces. Changing three symbols into a line only happens, if they are followed by [Enter].

> **TIP**   The AutoCorrect list is shared across Microsoft Office programs. If a particular abbreviation in Word interferes with your work in another program, consider using the find and replace method discussed above for that word only, or turn off AutoCorrect in the other program.

Occasionally AutoCorrect and AutoFormat flake out and do not perform an expected substitution. Blame it on the full moon or programming error. Most of the time, these commands offer tremendous benefits in correcting common mistyping or providing shortcuts for hard to type characters. At the same time, the automatism and, shall we say, unyielding arrogance of the substitutions can also drive you nuts. Microsoft has done a tremendous job with their word list so that annoyances in regular correspondence stay at a minimum, but jargon and foreign words can cause problems.

Take for example a World War II caper that includes messages in German in an otherwise English text. A common abbreviation like "usw." will trigger the rule for capitalizing the first letter of a word, since Word considers the period the end of the previous sentence. Throw in some foreign words for color and the word "teh," Slovenian for "these," ends up as "the" before you know it. Jargon can lead to similar problems, such as Word insisting "gold lamé" is "lame." Though not used often, three symbols ending up as a line upsets many, when it does happen. The most loathed rule must be the one that converts straight quotes to smart quotes. Following typesetting rules, Word converts apostrophes to curly quotes. At times, for instance after an em dash, an opening quote appears instead of the closing one. More aggravating for many people is that Word replaces apostrophes to indicate possession ('s) or in contractions like "can't," too, even though it is an acceptable usage according to typesetting rules. To make matters worse, find and replace respects the same rule, so attempts to change apostrophes followed by one letter fail grand style. While avoidable in business writing, a novel with realistic sounding dialogue puts the writer between an apostrophe rock and a quote hard place. If you leave the rule on, contractions appear with quotes, but if you turn the rule off, apostrophes surround quotations within dialogue.

For the occasional annoyance, like a foreign word, Word lets you undo the last AutoCorrect or AutoFormat. If multiple substitutions took place, each undo reverses one of them. Word even provides a special undo function for use with the mouse, the **AutoCorrect Options** button, shown in Figure 3-1, a blue bar below the first letter of a changed word that expands into a lightning bold box when the mouse gets close to it.

Figure 3-1: AutoCorrect Options button

TIP   If the **AutoCorrect Options** button hiding text makes you tear your hair out, save your sanity and good looks and turn it off. Click on the blue bar, select **Control AutoCorrect Options** to open the AutoCorrect dialog box, then uncheck the **Show AutoCorrect Options buttons** box at the top.

Undoing an AutoCorrect or AutoFormat

AR: Click **Undo** ↶ on the **Quick Access Toolbar**.
BR/**MAC**: Click **Undo** ↺ on the **Standard Toolbar** or click **Edit | Undo**.

Hover with the cursor over a substitution.
A blue bar or the **AutoCorrect Options** button appears under the first character of the word.
Click the button and select **Undo** from the list.

```
Ctrl + Z or Alt + Backspace (MAC: Cmd + Z)
```

Going through the undo on every appropriate use of an apostrophe, however, is distracting and annoying. Deal with them in bulk, instead.
First, turn off the rule for smart quotes using the following procedure.

Changing AutoCorrect or AutoFormat options

AR: Click **File | Options | Proofing,** then the [AutoCorrect] button.
O07: Click **Office | Word Options | Proofing,** then the [AutoCorrect] button.
BR/**MAC**: Click **Tools | AutoCorrect**.
MAC: Click **Word | Preferences | AutoCorrect**.
The **AutoCorrect** dialog box appears.

For AutoFormat rules select **AutoFormat** or **AutoFormat As You Type** as appropriate. Check or uncheck rules as desired.

Hover with the cursor over a substitution.
A blue bar or the **AutoCorrect Options** button appears under the first character of the word. Click the button and select the rule from the list, or choose **Control AutoCorrect Options** to load the dialog box.

> **TIP**   Checking **Automatically use suggestions from the spelling checker** causes AutoCorrect to replace misspellings automatically, if only one entry from a dictionary matches, including any custom dictionaries in use (see 6.1).

An apostrophe substitution does not show the **AutoCorrect Options** button that normally gives you access to control the rule, so you must use the menu choices instead. Once in the **AutoCorrect** dialog box, select **AutoFormat As You Type**. The **AutoFormat** tab by itself governs the rules for using the AutoFormat function on previously written text, accessible Before Ribbon through **Format | AutoFormat**. After Ribbon you must add AutoFormat to the menu yourself, which tells you how seldom the command is used. Using it for bulk reformatting gives you no control over the changes. While you can step through each one individually, it is tedious on a long document. We will rely on find and replace instead, which follows the rules under **AutoFormat As You Type**.
Uncheck **"Straight quotes"** with **"smart quotes."**

Figure 3-2: Substituting single quotes with apostrophe

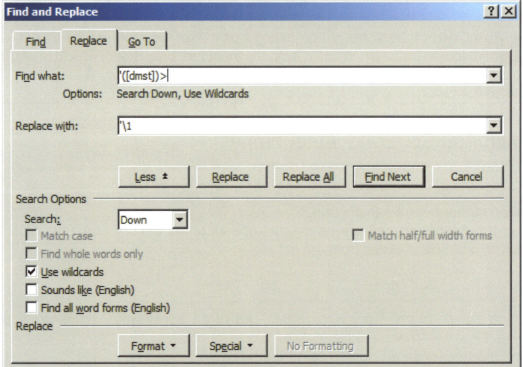

Replacing an apostrophe with itself now changes every single quote back to an apostrophe. Obviously, if we have dialogue containing single quotes, this is not desirable. Here we can finally use the mysterious wildcards discussed in chapter 1.6. Open the **Find and Replace** window, click [More], and check **Use wildcards**. Type '([dmst])>| in the **Find what** box. This string instructs word to look for a single quote followed by a single d, m, s, or t at the end of the word, thus finding the common uses of apostrophes for possession or in contractions. The wildcard find, unlike a regular find, distinguishes between quotes and apostrophes. For the above search to work, enter a single closing quote in the **Find what** box with [Ctrl] + ['], ['] (**MAC** Option + Shift +]) or copy and paste a closing quote from the text.

Type `\1` with a regular apostrophe for **Replace with**. This string tells Word to substitute the found text with an apostrophe followed by the found letter in the first parentheses, hence replacing it with itself, in the process replacing any quote with an apostrophe. The resulting dialog box is shown in Figure 3-2.

Click [Replace All] to apply the substitution. Other than the rare exception where a quote within dialogue begins with one of the four letters by itself, legitimate single quote marks remain untouched. A search and replace of `'([vr])e>` with `\1e` takes care of "'re" and "'ve." Finish off with a simple replace for `'ll`. If you want to continue using quote marks for quotations, check the rule in **AutoFormat As You Type** again.

Most of the AutoFormat rules are self-explanatory. Under **Apply as you type**, **Automated bulleted lists** reformats a line starting with *, -, or > followed by a space or tab to a bulleted list with a symbol, as if you had selected **Home | Bullets** in the **Paragraph** group (BR/MAC: **Format | Bullets and Numbering**). **Automatic numbered lists** similarly changes the style for a line starting with the number 1 followed by a period or tab. The change triggers when you end the line with [Enter]. To end the list hit [Enter] twice.

Border lines draws a line when you type the characters ~, #, *, -, or = three times in succession on a new line, then press [Enter]. Choosing **Home,** the *down triangle* ▾ next to **Borders** ⊞ in the **Paragraph** group, then **Borders and Shading** (BR/MAC: **Format | Borders and Shading**) produces the same effect. You may have encountered this behavior when using "***" on a line by itself as scene break. Using plus signs (+) instead avoids this issue. If you never use borders, save yourself the aggravation and turn off this rule.

> **TIP**   If you already have automatically generated borders running across the screen, getting rid of them can be challenging to say the least. Unlike other substitutions, borders are not text. Instead, they are an attribute of the paragraph, like line spacing. Turn on display of paragraph mark with **Show/Hide** ¶ , then select those around the line in turn and check for borders with **Home | Borders**. If the area has no text, a quicker way is to delete all surrounding paragraph marks and type in new blank lines. If text surrounds the line, cut a number of paragraphs to the clipboard and paste them back unformatted (see 1.5). The line should disappear. So will any text formatting, such as italics, so make sure to note these. You can always leave the original text in place, apply the formatting with the **Format Painter** ◆ to the unformatted copy, then delete the original text with the border afterwards.

Built-in Heading styles applies heading styles to paragraphs of five words or less that do not end with punctuation marks, after you press [Enter] twice. As is, Word applies the **Heading 1** style. Starting the lines with tabs applies a successively higher heading number. This option is off by default.

Tables lets you create tables with sequences of plus signs (+) and hyphens (-). If you use many tables, you may want to look up the specifics in Word Help.

Set left- and first-indent with tabs and backspaces indents paragraphs when you start a line with a tab. To ensure consistency and allow easy changes when converting a document to different ebook formats, you should *not* indent paragraphs individually, however. Apply a style instead.

Define styles based on your formatting applies one of the styles, if it matches the text's formatting. Usually you would want to control styles yourself to ensure consistency. This option is off by default, but can be useful, if you did not consistently apply styles to an existing text. You can then use the AutoFormat function to have Word search for and apply styles. The same caveat about loss of control from above applies just the same. If you are faced with going through the entire document to apply styles anyway, it at least can lessen the burden.

3.4.   *Writing with AutoCorrect*

Since AutoCorrect does nothing else but replace the word on the left of its built-in table with the phrase on the right, you can customize the substitutions to suit your own needs. Instead of typing abbreviations, then doing multiple find and replaces, enter them once in the AutoCorrect table. Whenever you finish an abbreviation with the space bar or most punctuation marks, Word instantly performs the substitution. Table 3-4 shows some samples.

> **TIP**   Word considers a single character followed by a period an initial. To trigger substitution of one character at the end of a sentence, hit the spacebar, then backspace, then period.

Table 3-4: Sample abbreviations for AutoCorrect

c	Cathrine
l	Carlisle
m	Tamalpais
p	President
dc	Washington, DC
la	Los Angeles
pa	parallel
mi	Mississippi
clt	couldn't
b	Bolívar
rsa	Reproduction Services Administration
fr	**Find and Replace window**
t	the
w	with
nv7	Las Vegas, NV 89107

Creating *unformatted* custom AutoCorrect entries

AR: Click **File** | **Options** | **Proofing,** then the [AutoCorrect] button.
O07: Click **Office** | **Word Options** | **Proofing,** then the [AutoCorrect] button.
BR/MAC: Click **Tools** | **AutoCorrect**.
MAC: Click **Word** | **Preferences** | **AutoCorrect**.
The **AutoCorrect** dialog box appears.
Type an abbreviation in the **Replace** box.
Type the substitution into the **With** box.
If the abbreviation already exists, click [Replace], otherwise click [Add].

Creating *formatted* custom AutoCorrect entries

To create a *formatted* entry, type it in Word and apply the desired formatting. Select the text, then do one of the following.
AR: Click **File** | **Options** | **Proofing,** then the [AutoCorrect] button.
O07: Click **Office** | **Word Options** | **Proofing,** then the [AutoCorrect] button.
BR/MAC: Click **Tools** | **AutoCorrect**.

MAC: Click **Word | Preferences | AutoCorrect**.
The **AutoCorrect** dialog box appears.
Type an abbreviation in the **Replace** box.
The plain text substitution should already appear in the **With** box.
Click the **Formatted text** button to include the formatting.
If the abbreviation already exists, click [Replace], otherwise click [Add].

Since the substitution takes place immediately when you end a word, you do not need to use special characters like the hash tag. AutoCorrect does have disadvantages compared to the find and replace method (FARM) discussed earlier. Since every entry in the table has to be a complete word, you must create separate substitution lines for variations of a word, such as plural form or past tense. For example, say you abbreviate "substitute" with "su." Whereas FARM replaces "#sus" with "substitutes," and "#sud" with "substituted," typing either one of them will not trigger an AutoCorrect substitution, since it expects to see the complete *word* "su." For frequently used words, you may want to enter variants, but often it is simpler to hit the space bar to end the word, then delete the space and type the needed letters.

Since plain text AutoCorrect does not allow wildcards like ^p in its list, to enter text that contains field codes, tabs or spans multiple lines, you must create it as a formatted entry as described above.

By judicious use of abbreviations, such as using single letters for common words like "the" and "with," you can cut down your typing considerably. Consider the following sample text, first as typed.

m stood at t wi behind her desk and searched for t sun wo luck. She raised her hands like a priestess worshipping t earth mo. "Be gone darkness, be gone. In t name of Gaia I demand sunshine for eo all t time." t clouds failed to yield. *What good is t Presidency, if I cnt command t weather, or b? At least I can do sth about this c l.*

"Sonia, find movie projs going into prod soon." She had named her cp in honor of one of her idols, Sonia Sotomayor, first Latina on t sc of t uns, long before t fe.

Word expanded the text as follows.

Tamalpais stood at the window behind her desk and searched for the sun without luck. She raised her hands like a priestess worshipping the earth mother. "Be gone darkness, be gone. In the name of Gaia I demand sunshine for everyone all the time." The clouds failed to yield. *What good is the Presidency, if I can't command the weather, or Bolívar? At least I can do something about this Cathrine Carlisle.*

"Sonia, find movie projects going into production soon." She had named her computer in honor of one of her idols, Sonia Sotomayor, first Latina on the Supreme Court of the United States, long before the Federation.

Keep in mind that one or two-letter abbreviations occasionally have uses, for example, "co" and "sc" as the state codes for "Colorado" and "South Carolina." Since Word considers an apostrophe a word boundary, any use of contractions or possessive triggers a substitution of the single letters "d," "m," "s," and "t." By replacing common contractions like "can't" or "wouldn't" with AutoCorrect entries of their own, you can avoid that issue and still use "t" as an abbreviation. You can always undo the substitution for the less common usages. The frequent use of the possessive "s," for most parts, precludes an AutoCorrect substitution for that letter. Table 3-5 gives a sample setup for common words, with particular emphasis on hard-to-type contractions common in fiction.

Table 3-5: Sample AutoCorrect entries for common words

aw	always
cnt	can't
cld	could
clt	couldn't
chg	change
cp	computer
cuz	because
dg	doing
dit	didn't
dnt	don't
dst	doesn't
eo	everyone
eg	for example
hnt	hadn't
hst	hasn't
hb	had been
ist	isn't
oc	of course
shd	should
sht	shouldn't
sth	something
t	the
th	there're
thg	things
tw	tomorrow
w	with
wh	which
wnt	won't
wld	would
wlt	wouldn't
hd	he'd
sd	she'd
td	they'd
hl	he'll
sl	she'll
tl	they'll
il	I'll
hs	he's
ss	she's
yr	you're
tr	they're
wr	we're

There is nothing wrong, of course, in using both FARM and AutoCorrect in the same manuscript. I have my standard list of AutoCorrect abbreviations set up and use them in all my writing. Terms that I use only in one chapter, for example "#fr" for "**Find and Replace**

window," I do through FARM, since I would have forgotten the abbreviation by the next time I work on the chapter, anyway. Furthermore, since Word maintains a single AutoCorrect list, the substitutions trigger in all documents, whereas I can create custom FARM macros for each file.

TIP   Word stores the unformatted AutoCorrect list in a file with a name including the language id and an extension **.ACL**, for example **MSO1033.ACL** for American English installations. Formatted entries are stored in the template **Normal.dotm** (Normal.dot in earlier versions). To use your custom list on another computer, search your source computer for these files using the search functions of the operating system like Explorer or Finder. Rename the existing files on the other computer, then copy over the ones from your original computer. *You will lose any customizations done on the destination computer.* If the computers do *not* use the same version of Word, you need to go through a transfer of the settings. Check the Microsoft web site for detailed instructions for both procedures.

For Windows versions the files are usually in
C:\Documents and Settings*username*\Application Data\Microsoft\Office *or* Templates

O13: C:\Users*username*\AppData\Local *or* Roaming\Microsoft\Templates

MAC Word 2011 for Mac stores *all* AutoCorrect entries in the Normal.dotm template, hence you cannot move entries in the .ACL file to the Mac. You can move Normal.dotm, which is usually in

/Users/~/Library/Application Support/Microsoft/Office/User Templates
To type the path in Finder hit [Cmd] + [Shift] + [G].

3.5. *Writing with AutoText*

Microsoft Word offers another choice for expanding abbreviations called AutoText that gives you more control. Unlike AutoCorrect, you have discretion whether a substitution takes place. You can select an AutoText entry from a list, or, if you type enough of the beginning of an entry for Word to recognize it, a pop-up balloon help appears offering the whole text. Try it out by typing "to w" on a new line. Word guesses that you want "To Whom It May Concern:" and offers that to you as an AutoComplete entry.

Inserting an AutoText entry
Type the beginning of the phrase.
Once the AutoComplete balloon help for the entry appears, hit [Enter] to insert it.
Some entries only trigger at the beginning of a new line.

Click **All Entries** on the AutoText toolbar.

AR: Click **Insert | Quick Parts** (Text group) | **Building Blocks Organizer** | **Gallery**.
BR/MAC: Click **Insert | AutoText**.
Select an entry from the gallery or menu, or AutoText to see all entries in a single list.

Creating an AutoText entry
Type the text in Word and apply the desired formatting.
Select the text, then do one of the following.
AR: Click **Insert | Quick Parts** (Text group) | **AutoText**.
BR/MAC: Click **Insert | AutoText | AutoText**.

Click the **AutoText** button on the AutoText toolbar or the **Create AutoText** button, available as customization for the Ribbon.
The **AutoCorrect** dialog box appears, displaying the text on the **AutoText** tab.
Click [Add].
You can also type unformatted entries directly in the **Enter AutoText entries here** box.

Since AutoText requires typing at least four characters, the default list consists mainly of longer building blocks for form letters, such as salutations and signature lines. Microsoft includes single words, too. Similar to AutoCorrect, you can embed field codes, such as the current date or page number, in entries by including them in the text you select before invoking AutoText. Which method you use to speed up your typing is more a matter of preference, and of course, you can mix methods as you please.

Since AutoComplete triggers based on the beginning of the words, it does poorly with variants of short words, such as "could" and "couldn't," whereas AutoCorrect can use different abbreviations. As Word maintains separate lists, however, you can use AutoCorrect for one alternative and AutoText for another. For example, you can define the abbreviation "co" in AutoCorrect as "company," and add "companies" to the AutoText list. Finally, since AutoText is stored in the template, you can have multiple versions for different projects, whereas the AutoCorrect list for unformatted entries is the same for all documents of one language.

4. Fields

Microsoft Word uses fields for information that can change, such as dates, or list and page numbers. Some, such as the table of contents, can create complex text spanning multiple lines.

4.1. Inserting Fields

You can insert any of the available fields using the **Field** dialog box. Word also has shortcuts for many of the most common items.

Inserting a field

AR: Click **Insert | Quick Parts** (Text group) | **Field**.
BR/MAC: Click **Insert | Field**.
In the **Field** dialog box select a field from the **Field names** list and select any options.
Click [OK].

```
Ctrl + F9 (MAC: Cmd + F9)
```

Inserting a date field in text

AR: Click **Insert | Date & Time** (Text group).
BR/MAC: Click **Insert | Date & Time**.
In the **Date & Time** dialog box select a format from the list.
Check the **Update automatically** box.
Click [OK].

```
Alt + Shift + D (MAC: Ctrl + Shift + D)
```

Inserting a date field in header or footer

Enter the header or footer (see Headers and Footers).
AR: Click **Header & Footer Tools Design | Insert | Date & Time**.
BR: On the **Header & Footer** toolbar click **Insert Date**.
MAC: Click **Header & Footer | Date** (Insert group).

```
Alt + Shift + D (MAC: Ctrl + Shift + D)
```

Inserting a page number

AR: Click **Insert | Page Number** (Header & Footer group).
BR/MAC: Click **Insert | Page Numbers**.
Select the placement on the page.
Click [OK].

```
Alt + Shift + P (MAC: Ctrl + Shift + P)
```

Properly formatted ebooks require additional specialized fields to allow hyperlinking within the document. To allow jumping to a location, insert a bookmark. When you then select text and convert it into a hyperlink, the reader can jump to the named bookmark by holding [Ctrl] and clicking the link.

Inserting a bookmark

Place the cursor where you want the bookmark.
AR: Click **Insert | Bookmark** (Links group).
BR/MAC: Click **Insert | Bookmark**.

```
Ctrl + Shift + F5 (MAC: Cmd + Shift + F5)
```
Enter a name for the bookmark.
Click [Add].

Inserting a hyperlink

Select the text you want to convert into a hyperlink.
AR: Click **Insert | Hyperlink** (Links group).
BR/MAC: Click **Insert | Hyperlink**.

```
Ctrl + K (MAC: Cmd + K)
```
If you did not select anything, type the text you want displayed for the hyperlink.
For a link to an external document or web page click **Existing File or Web Page** and select the destination. Include "http://" in front of web addresses as some ebook formats require it.
For a link within the document click **Place in This Document** and select a heading or bookmark from the list.
Click [OK].

4.2.   Editing Fields

Word automatically updates some fields. A few, such as page numbers and table of contents, involve considerable work, like repaginating the document. To avoid disrupting your writing, Word only updates these fields on demand.

Updating a field result

Click anywhere within the field then do one of the following.

```
F9 (MAC: Cmd + Option + Shift + U)
```
Right-click and select **Update Field.**

> **TIP**   To update all field results in a document, select all the text with [Ctrl] + [A], then press [F9].

> **TIP**   To force Word to update all field results every time you print a document, check the printing option **Update fields** under **Options | Display** (**BR**: **Tools | Options | Print; MAC**: **Word | Preferences | Print**).

At times, you may need to change the behavior of fields.

Editing a field

Click anywhere within the field.
Right-click and select **Edit Field** (not available for **Mac**).

The **Field** dialog box opens to allow updating the options for the field.

Editing the field loads the generic **Field** dialog box. If you prefer using the specialized dialog box for the field, select it and use the insert functions discussed above to replace the field with one that has the options you want.

Although they are not regular text, you can edit most fields by typing, once you have toggled to field code view. The Microsoft web site has extensive documentation on the many options you can set by changing the field code directly.

Switching between a field code and its result

Click anywhere within the field then do one of the following.

`[Shift] + [F9]`

Right-click and select **Toggle Field Codes.**

Switching between all field codes and their result

AR: Click **File | Options | Advanced**.
O07: Click **Office | Word Options | Advanced**.
Check the **Show field codes instead of their values** box in the **Show document content** section.

BR: Click **Tools | Options | View**.
MAC: Click **Word | Preferences | View**.
Check the **Field codes** box in the **Show** section.

> **TIP** Some fields are hidden, for example index markers. If you do not see a field, toggle **Show/Hide** ¶ (see 1.2).
>
> **TIP** To convert a field to regular text, select it and press `[Ctrl] + [Shift] + [F9]`. Unlike toggling the view, this step is irreversible, except for using **Undo**.

4.3.   Table of Contents

The table of contents is one of the most powerful fields a writer can use. The built-in choices by default gather up any lines with the first three heading styles. Figure 4-1 shows the table of contents for this book with the field code for one line visible. Word for Windows assembles a complex result out of standard building blocks. For each heading it adds a bookmark in the form "_Toc" followed by a number. The table itself contains a hyperlink field for each entry that jumps to the bookmark. The switch "/l" specifies a location in the document, as opposed to another file. The text displayed consists of the heading, in this case with the defined outline numbering, followed by a tab and the page number right-aligned. The look of each entry, such as the indentation and tab leader, follows a built-in style named "toc" with a number matching the heading level. Hence **Heading 1** uses **TOC 1**. Rather than individually changing the common formatting, like the tab leader, manage the table of contents as a whole through its dialog box.

> **TIP** If none of the built-in table of contents formats strike your fancy, you can quickly change the many styles and still ensure consistency by selecting the entire table and applying any format changes to all lines. Since the **TOC** styles are marked to update automatically, Word applies the changes to all the ones in use in the table.

Figure 4-1: Table of contents with hyperlink field code

Inserting a table of contents

Place the cursor where you want the table of contents.
AR: Click **Reference | Table of Contents** (Table of Contents group) | **Insert Table of Contents** or select an automatic one from the gallery.
BR: Click **Insert | Reference | Index and Tables | Table of Contents**.
MAC: Click **Document Elements**, then select a built-in one from the gallery.

MAC: Click **Insert | Index and Tables | Table of Contents**.

Modifying a table of contents' formatting

Place the cursor in an existing table of contents.
AR: Click **Reference | Table of Contents** (Table of Contents group) | **Insert Table of Contents**.
BR: Click **Insert | Reference | Index and Tables | Table of Contents**.
MAC: Click **Insert | Index and Tables | Table of Contents**.

Place the cursor *at the beginning of the first entry of the table of contents*.
Right-click and select **Edit Field**.
Click [Table of Contents].

The dialog box shown in Figure 4-2 changes the look of the table of contents in a consistent way. Clearing **Show page numbers** turns off the page numbers. Clearing **Right align page numbers** forces them to follow the text with just a space in between. When right aligned, the **Tab leader** specifies the characters used to connect the page numbers to the text on the left. **Show levels** governs how many heading levels Word includes. The **Formats** drop-down list allows you to select from one of six built-in formats or the styles included with the current template. The **Print Preview** pane displays how the table will look like when printed.

Clearing the **Use hyperlinks instead of page numbers** check box prevents Word for Windows from creating hyperlinks in the document. You may want to do so, if your entries include intricate formatting that the hyperlink style overrides. Since it deprives you of using the table of contents to navigate to a heading by ctrl-clicking it, you may want to hold off this step until you finished editing.

The [Modify] button lets you change the styles used with the table, a handy shortcut, since Word does not show them in the **Styles** task pane, unless you change the display options.

Figure 4-2: Index and Tables dialog box, Table of Contents pane

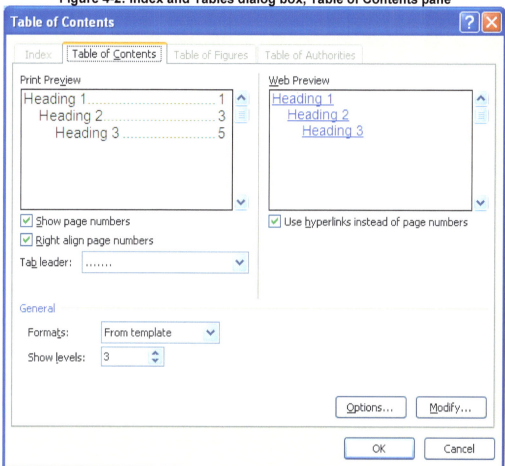

Word 2007 introduced automatic table of contents, selectable from its gallery. They have all the features of their predecessors, plus add a title and a frame with buttons to update and remove the table. To replace an existing old-style table of contents with the new version, you must save the document in the new DOCX format. Next, delete the existing table using the Before Ribbon method shown below and insert a new automatic one.

Removing a table of contents

AR: Place the cursor in an existing table of contents.
Click **Reference** | **Table of Contents** (Table of Contents group) | **Remove Table of Contents**.

AR (automatic only): Place the cursor in an existing automatic table of contents.
Click the **Table of Contents** buttons above the table title, then **Remove Table of Contents**.

BR: Place the cursor *at the beginning of the first entry of the table of contents*.
Select the entire table by pressing [Delete], [F8] twice, or dragging with the mouse.
[Delete]

Since updating the table of contents requires Word to gather all headings and repaginate the document, it does not do so automatically. You can update the table like any other field with the methods in 4.2, or use the buttons in the Ribbon and at the top of the automatic table of contents.

To minimize the effort involved, Word asks whether you want to update only the page numbers or the text, too. If you changed headings or other elements that impact the displayed text, select **Update entire table**. Since Word replaces all the text, any formatting not saved to an appropriate style is lost. To keep formatting for one line, use the TC fields described below.

Updating a table of contents

AR: Click **Reference** | **Table of Contents** (Table of Contents group) | **Update Table**.

AR (automatic only): Place the cursor in an existing automatic table of contents. Click the **Update Table** buttons above the table title.

Place the cursor in an existing table of contents.

```
[F9]  (MAC: [Cmd] + [Option] + [Shift] + U)
```

Clicking the [Options] button lets you specify text with custom styles to include in the table of contents. Checking **Outline levels** gathers all lines with styles that specify an **Outline Level** in their Paragraph formatting, including headings. For instance, the "Introduction" chapter uses **Title,** a level 1 style, thus forcing its inclusion in the table without interfering with the numbering of the headings. The Microsoft Office web site http://office.microsoft.com has detailed instructions, including videos, if you wish to pursue this advanced topic. Checking **Table entry fields** includes text within the TC fields described below.

Word allows multiple tables of contents in a document. Despite their name, you can use them for other purposes. A separate tab in the **Index and Tables** dialog box inserts a table of figures, which uses the \a switch to gather all captions with the word "figure" in them. The misleading tab name notwithstanding, changing the **Caption label** creates a table of tables or a table of equations.

You can roll your own table of what-ever-you-wants by adding hidden TC fields. Using the method shown in 4.1, insert them *before* the text or object to include, type a phrase to display in the table, and select the other options. Unless you specify a single-letter table identifier, the entry will appear in the main table of contents, which has an identifier of "C." Turn on the display of hidden text as discussed in 1.2 to edit the TC fields.

> **TIP**   To open a **Mark Table of Contents Entry** dialog box with limited options press `[Alt]` `+ [Shift] + [O]` (**MAC**: `[Cmd] + [Option] + [Shift] + O`).

For additional tables, create them with only a \f switch to gather matching entries. I created this book's table of tables using the code {TOC \f T} to maintain the color of the **Windows** and **Mac** entries in the print version. Whereas Word formats the text it gathers from headings and captions using the styles assigned to that level, it keeps the formatting of TC fields. The following field code adds an entry at the first indentation level to the table with the identifier "T." Notice the quotes around the phrase to ensure that more than the first word shows in the table.

{ TC "Cursor movement keys (**Mac**)" \f T \l "1" }

You can also use TC fields to include entries in the table of contents that you do not wish to format as headings or include in the outline levels. The following entry adds my contact information to the main table of contents.

{ TC "Contact Information" \l 1 \f C }

> **TIP** To restrict the table of contents to only a portion of a book, such as a chapter, select the text, then create a bookmark from it. Add the bookmark name to the TOC field code with a /b switch. Word only gathers headings in the bookmarked area.

The complexity of a table of contents can cause problems when moving from one version of Word to another. If you find glitches after an upgrade, save the document as a new format and replace the table of contents.

Just as Word has issues, so do ebook publishing services. In addition, since the ebook reader determines the pagination, the page numbers from Word have no meaning. Some hence recommend replacing the table of contents with handcrafted bookmarks and hyperlinks instead. You can still use the TOC fields until you are ready to publish, then use a copy trick to create a starting point. Turn off page numbers in the **Index and Tables** dialog box. If you copy the entire table of contents, Word places only one TOC field. By excluding the first line, you force Word to paste individual hyperlinks instead. Select the *second* through last line of the table of contents and press [Shift] + [F9]. Copy and paste the resulting hyperlink field codes below the existing table. Add an entry for the first line and you have all the hyperlink entries with minimal effort. If you prefer more meaningful bookmarks than "_toc," create your own for each heading, then edit the hyperlink field codes to match.

4.4. *Index*

What the table of contents does up front, the index does in the back, and it works the same way. Hidden fields tag keywords on each page. Another field gathers them into an index with page numbers. You force an update with [F9] and modify styles from the familiar **Index and Tables** dialog box shown in Figure 4-2 to change its appearance. Nothing could be simpler, right? Not quite. To create an index you need to mark, on every page, the words to include.

Marking an index entry

Select the phrase you want to mark.
AR: Click **Reference | Mark Index** (Index group).
BR: Click **Insert | Reference | Index and Tables | Index**, then click the [Mark Index] button.
MAC: Click **Insert | Index and Tables | Index**, then click the [Mark Index] button.

Alt] + [Shift] + [X] (**MAC**: [Cmd] + [Option] + [Shift] + X)
Pick the desired options in the **Mark Index Entry** dialog box, then click [Mark].
A hidden index entry field appears at the point of the cursor.
You can continue selecting and marking text without closing the dialog box.

The **Mark Index Entry** dialog box, shown in Figure 4-3, lets you specify what words to include in the index and how. The **Main entry** always appears first, in this case "Word." Words in the **Subentry** field appear indented, with every colon (:) adding an indent level. The Cross-reference option refers to another entry in the index, by default preceded by "*See,*" instead of giving a page number.

> **TIP** Since the index entry field is hidden, you can add one for words not displayed on the page by simply typing the text in the **Main entry** field.

The check boxes for **Bold** and **Italic** allow formatting the page numbers. To format the entries, select the text, right-click it and select **Font** from the menu. Pressing the [Mark] button inserts one field code at the cursor location.

Figure 4-3: Mark Index Entry dialog box

Mark Index Entry	? X

Index

Main entry: `Word`

Subentry: `Index:Mark`

Options

○ Cross-reference: `See`

◉ Current page

○ Page range

  Bookmark: `OLE_LINK1` ▼

Page number format

☑ Bold

☐ Italic

This dialog box stays open so that you can mark multiple index entries.

Mark	Mark All	Close

The above example produces the following field code that creates a three level index with the word "Index" and the page number in bold.

{ XE " Word:**Index**:Mark" \b }

The \t switch creates a cross-reference instead, as the following example show.

{ XE "**Microsoft Word**" \t "*see* **Word**" }

You can modify the field code directly and apply any additional formatting, instead of going through the dialog box. Turn on the display of hidden text as discussed in 1.2 to see the XE fields, then use the special find and replace string ^d xe (see 1.6) to look for them.

Deleting an index entry

Turn on the display of hidden text as discussed in 1.2, if needed.

Place the cursor at the beginning of the field, to the left of the opening curly brace ({).

Use `[Shift] + [right arrow]` or drag the mouse to the right to select the entire field including the closing curly brace (}).

`[Delete]`

When you insert an index field, Word gathers all the marked entries, sorts them alphabetically, adds page numbers, removes duplicates from the same page, and displays the result as an index. Figure 4-4 shows the result as a two-column Index with "Fancy" selected in the **Formats** list.

Figure 4-4: Sample Index

M¶	W¶
Microsoft·Word.· *See·*Word¶ MS·Word,·56¶	Word.·*See·*MS·Word¶ Index¶ Mark,·56¶

Inserting an index

Place the cursor where you want the index.
AR: Click **Reference** | **Index** (Index group) | **Insert Index** or select an automatic one from the gallery.
BR: Click **Insert** | **Reference** | **Index and Tables** | **Index**.
MAC: Click **Insert** | **Index and Tables** | **Index**.

Modifying an index's formatting

Place the cursor in an existing index.
AR: Click **Reference** | **Index** (Index group) | **Insert Index**.
BR: Click **Insert** | **Reference** | **Index and Tables** | **Index**.
MAC: Click **Insert** | **Index and Tables** | **Index**.

Place the cursor in an existing index.
Right-click and select **Edit Field**.
Click [Index].

Removing an index

Place the cursor in an existing index.
Select it by pressing [F8] five times or dragging with the mouse.
Press [Delete].

> **TIP**   Selecting a large index with the mouse can be tedious. Instead, toggle to the field code (see 4.2) and select the one line instead.

Checking **Right align page numbers** moves them to a right-aligned tab stop connected to the text with the character specified by the optional **Tab leader**. The **Formats** drop-down list allows you to select from one of six built-in formats or the styles included with the current template. The **Print Preview** pane displays how the table will look like when printed.
The **Type** buttons govern how Word treats subentries. The default, **Indented**, produces the result in the sample above with one entry per line. The **Run-in** choice instead bunches the entries together, separated by colons and semi-colons. The built-in formats create two-columns of indexes, easily changeable with the **Columns** option.
The [Modify] button lets you change the styles used with the index, a handy shortcut, since Word does not show them in the **Styles** task pane, unless you change the display options. Each level has its own associated style named "Index" followed by a number. As with the table of contents, use the options in the dialog box to achieve a consistent format for all entries and only change individual styles in rare occasions.

> **TIP**   If none of the built-in index formats strike your fancy, you can quickly change the many styles and still ensure consistency by selecting the entire index and applying any format changes to all lines. Since the **Index** styles are marked to update automatically, Word applies the changes to all the ones in use in the index.

Most of the time you want all occurrences of a phrase tagged. The [Mark All] button in the **Mark Index Entry** dialog box marks *all* occurrences of an *exact* match of the **Main entry** phrase by placing index entry fields *after* them. The [Mark All] button may only activate if you select text before opening the dialog box. Typing into an empty **Main entry** field sometimes does not activate the button. This seems to be a bug.

Figure 4-5: Index and Tables dialog box, Index pane

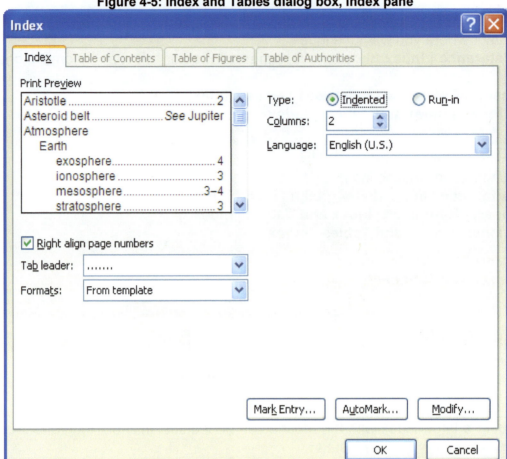

As the match is exact, you must repeat the procedure with any alternate spellings you want indexed, including plural forms and capitalized versions that may occur at the beginning of a sentence. Hence, to mark all occurrences of "heading" or "headings," for example, requires four passes: singular upper- and lowercase, and plural upper- and lowercase. Just like with a table of contents, you can restrict the search to a part of the document by selecting all the text to include and inserting a bookmark for it, then specifying the bookmark as **Page range**.

At this point, you may be thinking of your jillion-page masterpiece requiring quadjillion index entries that you painstakingly have to mark with the dialog box four different ways. Before you run screaming out the door after flinging your computer out the window, consider the [AutoMark] button in the **Index and Tables** dialog box. By specifying a concordance file with AutoMark, you can have Word mark all phrases listed in the file at once.

As shown in Figure 4-6, a concordance file is a Word document containing only a two-column table. In some versions of Microsoft Word, AutoMark searches only require a complete match to the phrase on the left. Hence, "heading" also covers "headings." To be safe, include the plural form anyway. AutoMark adds an index- entry field code with the phrase on the right, including any formatting. As the "**AutoCorrect**" example shows, if the search phrase is what you want displayed in the index, you can leave the right side blank. AutoMark copies the search phrase including any formatting to the field code. You can create subentries with colons. The complete-match rule means that I can distinguish between the Normal style, always capitalized in this book, and the word "normal." You must specify both upper- and lowercase forms, if you want them both indexed.

Figure 4-6: Sample concordance table

Interface	**interface**
find and replace	**find and replace**
go to	**go to**
browse	**browse**
style	**styles**
Normal.dot	**template**
Normal	**Styles**:Normal
AutoCorrect	
field code	
heading	**Styles**:heading
Heading	**Styles**:heading
shortcut	keyboard shortcuts

TIP   AutoMark can make hundreds of changes to your document. Consider experimenting on a copy instead of the original.

Although the concordance file takes care of most of the work, some clean-up remains. While the entry for "Normal," for instance, ignores any lowercase version of the word, it finds the uppercase version in "Normal.dot" just the same, tagging it as both a template and a style. For special cases like this, you must search for any incorrectly placed fields and delete them.

AutoMark also searches all text, happily tagging any occurrences in appendixes or preliminary materials like the table of contents. Unless you want these pages included in the index, delete the extraneous field codes. Obviously, updating a table of contents with one of the methods shown in 4.2 wipes out all the index entry fields in it all at once.

AutoMark cannot create cross-references. You need to add them yourself. Since Word does not care where you place a cross-reference, because it has no page numbers associated with it, you can gather all of them together on a blank page at the end of the document. Aggregating them in this way allows you to easily copy and save them, should you have to wipe out all index entry fields as discussed below.

TIP   Although hidden, index fields on blank pages by themselves still generate blank pages when printed. To minimize wasted pages bunch them together without carriage returns and reduce the font.

Invariably, documents and concordance files are updated. When re-running AutoMark, it will not delete fields where the phrase in the field has changed in the concordance file from the last pass, even if only the formatting differs. For example, if I change the bold "**interface**" to regular "interface," the field codes with bold text remain in the document and, since they come first, will still create a bold index entry. Do not scream at the wall or throw your computer out the window. Instead, jump to the beginning of your document, open your trusted **Find and Replace** dialog box (see 1.6), and enter the string ^d xe ^? in **Find what**. Include the spaces around the "xe." The special characters instruct Word to search for a field starting with a space, then "xe," then another space, followed by any character. The search automatically selects an entire field all the way to the closing curly brace, as you can easily test by pressing [Find Next]. Leave the **Replace with** field blank and make sure **Match case** is not checked. Pressing [Replace All] causes Word to search the entire document for index entry fields and replace them with nothing, giving you a clean slate to start over with a concordance file. This drastic method removes *all* index entry fields, even those you created manually, such as cross-references. Make a copy of the document, just in case. If you grouped all the cross-references together, as recommended above, you can copy them from the backup after the replace.

Since updating the index requires Word to gather all fields and repaginate the document, it does not do so automatically. You can update the index like any other field with the methods in 4.2, or use the button in the Ribbon. Since Word replaces all the text, any formatting not saved to an appropriate style is lost. To keep formatting for one line, format the XE field as described above.

Updating an index

AR: Click **Reference** | **Index** (Index group) | **Update Index**.

Place the cursor in an existing index.

[F9] (MAC: [Cmd] + [Option] + [Shift] + [U])

5. Page Setup

So far, we have dealt with text. Pages make a book, however. This chapter deals with their appearance. The **Draft** or **Normal View** (see 1.7) lets you focus on the text. To make the remaining page elements visible, switch to **Print Layout View**. The screen now displays the page in its defined size with the page elements like margins, header, and footer similar to Figure 5-1. The example shows two pages of this book, letter size (8.5x11 inches), portrait orientation (short edge at the top), mirror margins with extra gutter space on the inside for binding, but otherwise uniform margins. A section break separates the preliminary materials and body to allow changing the page number format from Roman to regular numerals and restarting the page numbering at one.

Figure 5-1: Letter-size portrait page design with mirror margins

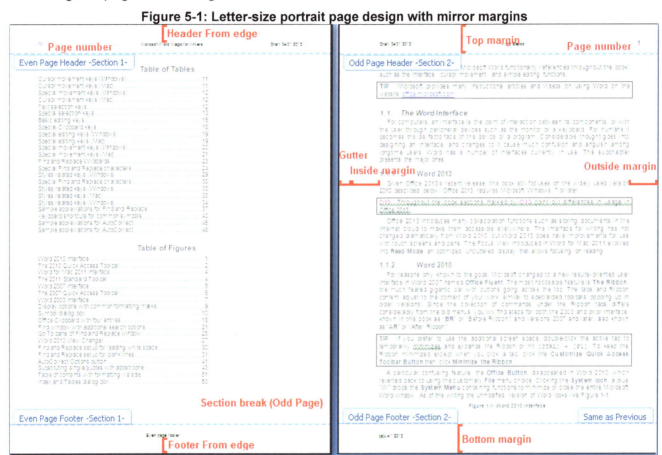

5.1.   Size and Margins

By default, Word creates a new document in the most common print size for the region, "letter" for the USA, or "A4" for Western Europe. You may want to leave this size during the editing process for print outs for critiquing and submissions to agents, since many printers produce unexpected results with non-standard paper sizes.

Many publishing services provide pre-formatted Word templates for different print sizes. When copying the text of your book into the template, Word adjusts the content to the correct page design, provided the template contains all the right settings. Some elements, particularly headers and footers, described below, may require changes. You can also modify the page design yourself. When changing the paper size, make sure to adjust margins and tab stops to match the new layout.

Changing page size

AR: Click **Page Layout | Size** (Page Setup group).
AR: Click **Page Layout |** *Page Setup dialog launcher* ⃞ (the tiny arrow in the bottom right corner of the **Page Setup** group), then select the **Paper** tab.
BR: Click **File | Page Setup**, then select the **Paper** tab.
MAC: Click **File | Page Setup**.
MAC: Click **Layout | Size** (Page Setup group).
Select a **Paper size**.

Changing page orientation

AR: Click **Page Layout | Orientation** (Page Setup group).
AR: Click **Page Layout |** *Page Setup dialog launcher* ⃞ (the tiny arrow in the bottom right corner of the **Page Setup** group), then select the **Margins** tab.
BR: Click **File | Page Setup**, then select the **Margins** tab.
MAC: Click **File | Page Setup**.
MAC: Click **Layout | Orientation** (Page Setup group).
Select an **Orientation**.

> **TIP**   Many **Page Setup** (**MAC**: **Document**) dialog box panes have an **Apply to** drop-down list at the bottom. For changes to the entire book make sure the entry is set to **Whole document**.

You can create your own paper size by selecting **More Paper Sizes** from the gallery, then **Custom size** from the list in the **Page Setup** dialog box. Specify the **Width** and **Height** in the fields below the list.

> **TIP**   Word does not allow saving custom paper sizes with a name, but it includes the ones specified by the current printer driver. Most publishing services accept PDF files. PDF printer drivers often let you create and save custom paper sizes that you can then use in Word.

When you change paper size, Word does *not* automatically adjust the margins, the blank space between the paper edge and the text. A standard one-inch margin, appropriate for submissions on letter-size paper, wastes considerable space in a five-by-eight-inches book. Also, by default Word assumes you will print single-sided with specified left and right margins, and possibly extra space on the left, called a gutter, for three-hole punching. Bound books require mirror margins with a gutter on the inside to ensure the same amount of space from the edge on both sides.

Changing margins

AR: Click **Page Layout | Margins** (Page Setup group).
AR: Click **Page Layout |** *Page Setup dialog launcher* ⃞ (the tiny arrow in the bottom right corner of the **Page Setup** group), then select the **Margins** tab.
BR: Click **File | Page Setup**, then select the **Margins** tab.
MAC: Click **File | Page Setup**, change **Settings** to Microsoft Word, then click [Margins].
MAC: Click **Layout | Margins** (Page Setup group).
Select margins from the gallery or enter new values for the four margins, and optionally for the gutter, in the **Page Setup** dialog box.

> **TIP**   The built-in margins in the gallery set the gutter to zero. Some publishing services' software requires a gutter value. If so, create custom margins, enter a number for the gutter, and subtract the same amount from the inside margin. The printout will look the same, and the software is happy.

For bound books select **Mirrored** from the gallery or create your own margins by selecting **Custom Margins** to load the **Page Setup** dialog box and change **Multiple pages** to **Mirror margins**.

> **TIP**   **Mirror margins** ensures that margins are a mirror image on the left page and the right page when printed to *two* separate sheets of paper. If you want to create a fold-over booklet with two pages printed on *one* sheet, select **Book fold** instead.

Shrinking margins may cut-off the headers or footers, the text in the margins containing information such as page numbers or the book title. Similar to the margins, the measurement goes from the edge to top of the header and the bottom of the footer, respectively.

Changing header or footer distance

AR: Click **Page Layout** | *Page Setup dialog launcher* ⌐ (the tiny arrow in the bottom right corner of the **Page Setup** group), then select the **Layout** tab.
BR: Click **File** | **Page Setup**, then select the **Layout** tab.
MAC: Click **File** | **Page Setup**, change **Settings** to Microsoft Word, then click [Margins].
MAC: Click **Layout** | **Margins** (Page Setup group).
Change the **From edge** values for **Header** or **Footer**.

While editing a header or footer.
AR: In **Header & Footer Tools**, change **Header from Top** or **Footer from Bottom** in the Position group.
BR: Load the **Page Setup** dialog box from the **Page Setup** button in the **Header and Footer** toolbar, then select the **Layout** tab.
MAC: Load the **Document** dialog box from the **Document Layout** button in the **Header and Footer** toolbar, then select the **Margins** tab.

To ensure that characters do not run into the body text, the difference between the top margin and the header distance value or the bottom margin and the footer distance value must exceed the font size. In desktop publishing, an inch has 72 PostScript points, making one point 0.0139 inches or 0.3527 mm. A 12-point character takes up 0.167 inches (4.2 mm), a 10-point character 0.139 inches (3.5 mm). As some letters, such as "g" and "p" lie below the line, the difference should be at least 0.2 inches (5 mm). The example in Figure 5-1 has 0.75-inch (19 mm) margins with header and footers 0.4 inches (10 mm) from the edges, leaving an ample 0.35 inches (9 mm) for the 0.11 inches high 8-point text.

5.2.   Headers and Footers

The headers or footers are separate parts of the document independent of the body text. They repeat on every page and commonly contain the page numbers, book or chapter titles, and author information.

Modifying headers or footers

AR: Click **Insert** | **Header** or **Footer** (Header & Footer group), select a built-in one from the gallery or **Edit** to create your own.

MAC: Click **Document Elements | Header** or **Footer** (Header & Footer group), then select a built-in one from the gallery.
BR/MAC: Click **View | Header and Footer**.

Double-click an existing header or footer.

When modifying headers or footers Word loads a separate **Header & Footer Tools Design** Ribbon or **Header and Footer** toolbar including buttons for inserting and formatting page numbers, dates, and navigating among headers or footers.

> **TIP**   The **Go to Header** and **Go to Footer** buttons in the **Header & Footer Tools Design** Ribbon (**BR**: **Switch Between Header and Footer** button in toolbar) let you switch even if the other one is not visible on screen.

Word allows up to three headers or footers, separate ones for the first and subsequent odd or even pages. As you can see in this book, the first page, the title page, has none. The even pages list the book title, whereas the odd pages show the chapter title.

Creating separate headers or footers for different pages

AR: Click **Page Layout** | *Page Setup dialog launcher* ⌐ (the tiny arrow in the bottom right corner of the **Page Setup** group), then select the **Layout** tab.
BR: Click **File | Page Setup**, then select the **Layout** tab.
MAC: Click **Format | Document**, then select the **Layout** tab
Check **Different odd and even** to create separate ones on even- and odd-numbered pages.
Check **Different first page** to create a separate one for the first page only.

While editing a header or footer.
AR/MAC: In **Header & Footer Tools Design**, check **Different odd and even** or **Different first page** in the Options group.
BR: Load the **Page Setup** dialog box from the **Page Setup** button in the **Header and Footer** toolbar, then select the **Layout** tab.
MAC: Load the **Document** dialog box from the **Document Layout** button in the **Header and Footer** toolbar, then select the **Layout** tab.

To ensure a consistent look and allow easy modification later, format every header and footer with the same style, such as **Header** or **Footer**. By default, both derive from the **Normal** style. If you make major changes, you can save yourself the extra formatting by deriving one from the other. For example, in this book the **Header** style uses an 8-point font and tabs specific to a letter-size page. The **Footer** style is based on **Header** and inherits those attributes.

> **TIP**   **BR**: The **Show Previous** and **Show Next** buttons in the **Header and Footer** toolbar let you move to the previous or next one, even if the other one is not visible on screen.

If your headers and footers contain only one centered item, modify the styles to align centered. If you want parts in the corners and in the middle, as is the case in this book, you must use **Center** and **Right** tab stops. Word includes them in the default formatting of headers and footers, although their placements may not be exactly where you want them. If you change page size later, you *must* adjust the tab stops to match, or header and footer elements will fall off the page or off-center. Consistently using styles avoids the need to change many, many headers and footers.
The text you type after a tab character centers around a **Center** tab stop. A **Right** tab stop pushes the text following a tab character to the left so that the last character aligns with the

stop. To change tabs place the cursor in the desired header or footer and load the **Tabs** dialog box. You can also manipulate tab stops directly using the horizontal ruler. For consistency among different headers and footers, change the tab stops in the **Modify Styles** dialog box instead by clicking the [Format] button and selecting **Tabs**.

Displaying the ruler
AR: Click **View | Ruler** (Show/Hide group).
BR/MAC: Click **View | Ruler**.

AR: Click the the **View Ruler** button consistency, you should make changes to the paragraph formatting of the appropriate style instead.on the far right, above the vertical scroll bar.

TIP The indent markers, move

Figure 5-2 shows a typical able triangles on the ruler, allow you to change indentation for the current paragraph. For horizontal ruler for a header. The **Tab Selector** on the left determines the alignment of the tab stop that clicking on the ruler sets. You can click and drag a tab stop to a new position and double-click a tab stop to bring up the **Tabs** dialog box for it. Since tab stops are a function of a line, clicking the vertical ruler does not place any.

Figure 5-2: Ruler for header

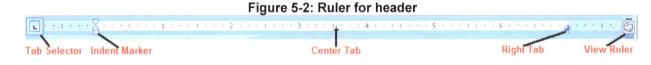

Tab Selector   Indent Marker   Center Tab   Right Tab   View Ruler

Creating a tab stop
AR: Click **Home** | *Paragraph dialog launcher* ⌐ (the tiny arrow in the bottom right corner of the **Paragraph** group), then click the [Tabs] button.
BR/MAC: Click **Format | Tabs**.
MAC: Click the **Tab Selector**, then select **Tabs**.
Enter a position as measured from the end of the left margin, i.e. the start of the body text.
Change **Alignment** and **Leader** as desired.
Click [Set]

Click the **Tab Selector** in the ruler until it displays the desired tab stop type.
Click the position in the horizontal ruler where you want the tab.

While editing a header or footer.
AR: In **Header & Footer Tools**, click **Insert Alignment Tab** in the Position group.

Moving a tab stop
AR: Click **Home** | *Paragraph dialog launcher* ⌐ (the tiny arrow in the bottom right corner of the **Paragraph** group), then click the [Tabs] button.
BR/MAC: Click **Format | Tabs**.
MAC: Click the **Tab Selector**, then select **Tabs**.
Click an existing tab stop in the list.
Enter a new position, **Alignment**, **Leader** as needed.
Click [Set]
Select the old tab stop in the list.
Click [Clear]

Click the tab stop in the ruler and drag it to the new position.

Modifying a tab stop

AR: Click **Home** | *Paragraph dialog launcher* ⌐ (the tiny arrow in the bottom right corner of the
Paragraph group), then click the [Tabs] button.
BR/MAC: Click **Format** | **Tabs**.
MAC: Click the **Tab Selector**, then select **Tabs**.
Click an existing tab stop in the list.
Change **Alignment** and **Leader** as desired.
Click [Set]

Double-click the tab stop in the ruler to load the **Tabs** dialog box.
Change **Alignment** and **Leader** as desired.
Click [Set]

Deleting a tab stop

AR: Click **Home** | *Paragraph dialog launcher* ⌐ (the tiny arrow in the bottom right corner of the
Paragraph group), then click the [Tabs] button.
BR/MAC: Click **Format** | **Tabs**.
MAC: Click the **Tab Selector**, then select **Tabs**.
Click an existing tab stop in the list.
Click [Clear]

Click the tab stop in the ruler and drag it down and off the ruler.

| TIP | If you accidentally move a tab stop or indent marker on the ruler, use **Undo** ↺ . |

Due to the prominence of page numbers in headers or footers, Word for Windows includes a
separate gallery to place preformatted, automatically updating page number fields accessible
through **Insert** | **Page Number** (Header & Footer group) or **Header & Footer Tools** | **Page
Number** (Header & Footer group). If starting new headers or footers, you can select pre-built
ones from **Top of Page** or **Bottom of Page**. Since these overwrite existing headers or footers,
if you want to preserve them, select a choice from **Current Position** instead. The **Page
Margins** gallery creates page numbers in frames in the *left* or *right* margins. These do not alter
existing headers or footers.

5.3.   Section Breaks

Just as a paragraph can only have one style, a simple document can only have one set of
three headers and footers. What to do, if you need to change the format of page numbers or
have different chapter titles in the header like in this book? In the olden days writers first ripped
out their hair, then assembled a book from subdocuments stored in different files. Fortunately,
Word offers a better way. Just as the style is stored in a paragraph mark, the page design is
stored in a hidden formatting mark called a section break. The last and often only one is stored
inside the document's last paragraph mark.
Similar to the paragraph mark, a section break controls the formatting of the text that *precedes*
it. And similar to paragraph marks, deleting a section break causes the preceding text to
assume the formatting of the *following* section.
You can change these formatting choices for individual sections, in addition to a number of
advanced features not covered in this book, in the **Page Setup** dialog box.

- Margins,
- Paper size or orientation,
- Headers and footers,
- Columns,
- Page numbering,
- Line numbering.

Inserting a section break

Place the cursor where you want the section break.
AR: Click **Page Layout | Break** (Page Setup group).
BR/MAC: Click **Insert | Break**.
MAC: Click **Layout | Break** (Page Setup group).
Select the section break type you want.

The type of section break determines the behavior of text *following* it. The **Next page** or **New page** type forces the following text onto the next page, a common choice for separating preliminary materials and body, or chapters in a book.
The **Continuous** type separates two sections on the same page, useful when you want different numbers of columns, for example. Tables achieve the same effect without the complexity of multiple sections, however. Since a single page cannot have two different page orientations or paper sizes, changing these two formatting options in one section forces a **Continuous** section break to become a **Next Page** one.
The **Even page** or **Odd page** types force the following text onto an even- or odd-numbered page, useful if you want chapters to always begin on an odd page, for example. If necessary, Word inserts a blank page when the document is printed.

Modifying a section break type

Place the cursor in the section *after* the break. (Unintuitive, but true)
AR: Click **Page Layout |** *Page Setup dialog launcher* ⌐ (the tiny arrow in the bottom right corner of the **Page Setup** group).
BR: Click **File | Page Setup**.
MAC: Click **Format | Document**.
Select the **Layout** Tab
Change **Section start** to the type you want.
Do not delete a section break and insert a different one or you will lose the section formatting for the text preceding the break.

The **Show/Hide button** ¶ (see 1.2) makes section and page breaks visible, but in **Print Layout View** text often hides them. In **Draft** or **Normal View** (see 1.7) section and page breaks always appear on a line by themselves, as shown in Figure 5-3.

Removing a section break

Change to **Draft** or **Normal View** (see 1.7).
Select a section break indicated by a double line and the words "Section Break."
`[Delete]`

Figure 5-3: Highlighted section break

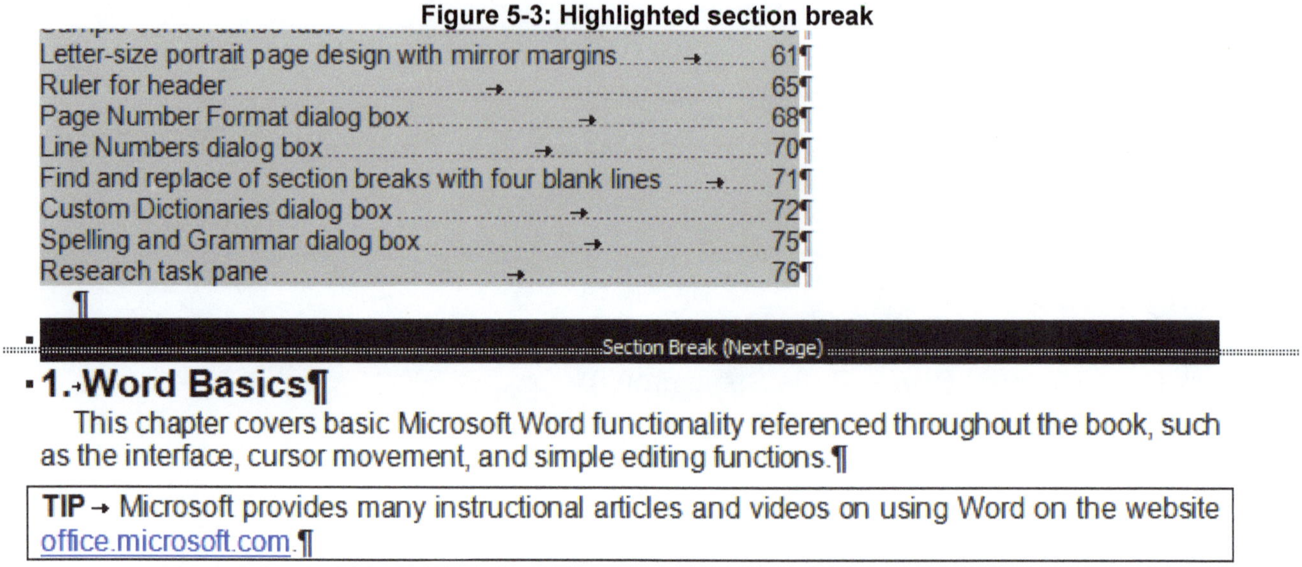

Letter-size portrait page design with mirror margins → 61¶
Ruler for header → 65¶
Page Number Format dialog box → 68¶
Line Numbers dialog box → 70¶
Find and replace of section breaks with four blank lines → 71¶
Custom Dictionaries dialog box → 72¶
Spelling and Grammar dialog box → 75¶
Research task pane → 76¶
¶
Section Break (Next Page)

1.→Word Basics¶

This chapter covers basic Microsoft Word functionality referenced throughout the book, such as the interface, cursor movement, and simple editing functions.¶

TIP→ Microsoft provides many instructional articles and videos on using Word on the website office.microsoft.com.¶

Do not confuse a section break with a page break. The latter forces a new page, nothing more. The page design does not change, only the page number goes up by one. In novels without chapter titles where the headers and footers remain the same, page breaks are appropriate to separate chapters. For consistency you should include them in the **Heading** styles by checking **Page break before** in the paragraph formatting (see 2.1.2), instead of inserting them manually each time you start a new chapter.

Inserting a page break

Place the cursor where you want the page break.
AR: Click **Page Layout** | **Break** (Page Setup group).
BR: Click **Insert** | **Break**.
MAC: Click **Layout** | **Break** (Page Setup group).
Select **Page** from the list.

`[Ctrl] + [Enter]`

`MAC: [Shift] + [Enter]` or `[Shift] + [Fn] + [Return]`

Removing a page break

Change to **Draft** or **Normal View** (see 1.7).
Select a page break indicated by a single line and the words "Page Break."
`[Delete]`

> **TIP** To see what section the current page is in, check the "**Sec**" or "**Section**" indicator in the **Status Bar** at the bottom of the Word screen. If the indicator is not visible, right-click the **Status Bar** to open the **Customize Status Bar** menu and click **Section**.

With one exception, the page formatting methods described apply to single- and multi-section documents. Most dialog boxes that apply section formatting contain a drop-down list labeled **Apply to**. Until you insert section breaks this setting defaults to **Whole document**. Once you break the text into sections, the default becomes **This section**. If you want to change page size or margins across the entire document, set this option to **Whole document** before hitting [OK], or you get to repeat the formatting for other sections. If you want to exclude earlier sections, for example, by changing the formatting of the page numbers only in the body, selecting **This point forward** will do the trick. If you select a range of sections first, Word also makes the choices **Selected sections** and **Selected text** available.

TIP   **This point forward** and **Selected text** automatically insert section breaks as necessary. If that is not what you want, make sure the cursor is at the beginning of a section and the highlight ends at a section break.

5.4. Using Sections

The most common use of sections in books is to change headers or footers and restart page and line numbering. This manual, for instance, uses Roman numerals for page numbers in the preliminary materials, then switches to regular numbers starting at "1-1" in the body. An odd-page section break separates each section so the page count can restart at one. In addition, odd pages have chapter titles in the header.

Figure 5-4: Page Number Format dialog box

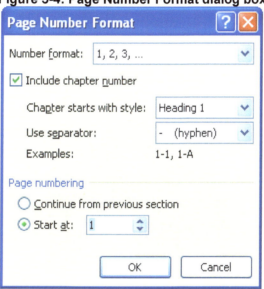

To change the page number format or restart it, Word has a **Page Number Format** dialog box, depicted in Figure 5-4. The **Number format** list lets you select the display format for the page numbers. If you marked chapter titles with a heading style (see 2.1.2), checking **Include chapter number** will precede each page number with the chapter numbers down to the level specified by the **Chapter starts with style**, separated by the character specified by **Use separator**. By default, Word uses a whole number based on the count of **Heading 1** and a dash as separator, so the first page of chapter one appears as "1-1."

Changing page numbers

Click on the page number you want to change.
AR: Click **Header & Footer Tools** | **Page Number** (Header & Footer group) | **Format Page Numbers**.
BR: On the **Header and Footer** toolbar click the **Format Page Numbers** button.

AR: Click **Insert** | **Page Number** (Header & Footer group) | **Format Page Numbers**.
BR/MAC: Click **Insert** | **Page Number**, then click the [Format] button.
Make the desired changes in the **Page Number Format** dialog box.

To aid editing you can turn on line numbering. Word places them into the left margin without disturbing the page design. Just like page numbers, you can restart line numbering in each section, even on each page, but the formatting is fixed at the Normal style font.

Changing line numbers

AR: Click **Page Layout | Line Numbers** (Page Setup group).
MAC: Click **Layout | Line Numbers** (Page Setup group).
Select a line number type from the list or **More Line Numbering/Line Numbering Options**.

AR: Click **Page Layout** | *Page Setup dialog launcher* ⌐ (the tiny arrow in the bottom right corner of the **Page Setup** group).
BR: Click **File | Page Setup**.
MAC: Click **Format | Document**.
Select the **Layout** Tab
Click the [Line Numbers] button.
Make the desired changes in the **Line Numbers** dialog box.

The **Line Numbers** dialog box, depicted in Figure 5-5, gives you considerable control over the numbering. Word will start at the number in **Start at** and increment the count by the value in **Count by**. The **From text** value specifies how much space to leave between the numbers and the text to their right. The higher the value the more the numbers move to the left without changing the left margin. The **Numbering** buttons allow you to restart the count at one on each page, at the beginning of the current section, or continue it from the previous section.

Figure 5-5: Line Numbers dialog box

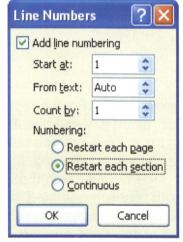

In books with chapter titles, such as this book, or story collections, sections allow you to change headers or footers to match the current content. Unlike page breaks, Word does not allow specifying a section break type in a style. You must insert them manually. Before you go hog-wild creating dozens of sections, get the page design finished first. The new section inherits the formatting from the current one, so it saves much effort to have common elements done beforehand. For instance, this book uses a common header on even pages and the same page-numbering format on all body pages. To minimize my effort, I modified the **Header** style, created a standard header with separate page number format using the **Page Number** style, set up mirrored pages, specified different odd and even headers, then copied the header and modified it, all before creating a section. Now, with every new chapter, I only have to insert an **Odd page** section break, unlink the header, and change the chapter title. The rest of the header remains the same. In reality, I do the header customizations before sending the manuscript for publishing, as forcing a new page ahead of every section break just wastes paper when making print outs for critiquing.

The unlink step is crucial. Word creates the headers and footers by linking them together for the two section. If you change the header or footer in one section, the other one automatically changes, too. This ensures consistency for the even-page header in this book, but does not work for the odd pages. By unlinking those, I can add separate chapter titles without affecting other sections. Since you now need to apply future changes to the header or footer formatting to all sections individually, I will repeat to *finish the page design before breaking the document into sections*.

Unlinking headers or footers

Place the cursor in the header or footer of the *second* section of the two that you want to unlink from each other.

AR: Click **Header & Footer Tools | Link to Previous**, if the button is not highlighted.

BR: On the **Header and Footer** toolbar click the **Link to Previous** button, if it is depressed.

> **TIP   AR**: The **Previous Section** and **Next Section** buttons in the **Header and Footer** Ribbon let you move to the previous or next sections, even if they are not visible on screen.

By turning on different first page, odd and even headers, footers, and unlinking them, you can create a total of six in each section and play with them to your heart's content. *The unlinking only affects one header or footer at a time. If you want to change all six, you must do the unlinking process six times*. Considering the effort of modifying them all, should, for example, a publisher ask for changes, even with judicious use of styles, think hard about whether you really need all the different ones. In the body, the first page of each section looks like the rest, so I dispensed with that option. The book does not have footers at all. To allow the page numbers to appear on the outside, I do have different headers for odd and even pages, but those on the even pages are all linked. In total, I have to manage three headers in the preliminary materials, one for all the even pages of the body, and an additional one for each section. Not too bad with a consistent use of styles.

Speaking of publishers, ebooks do not like page or section breaks, since the reader application handles the page formatting and decides on page breaks. Some conversion software understands the **Heading** styles and automatically applies its own page breaks before each heading. Others look for four blank lines. To prepare your document for submission, turn off page breaks in the **Heading** styles. Next, perform separate find and replaces for page and section breaks using the special characters ^m and ^b. To eliminate them, simply leave **Replace with** blank. If you need to keep some page breaks, replace them with four blank lines by using ^p^p^p^p. Since Word applies the style of the following paragraph, usually a heading, force the **Normal** style in the replace. Figure 5-6 shows the setup.

Figure 5-6: Find and replace of section breaks with four blank lines

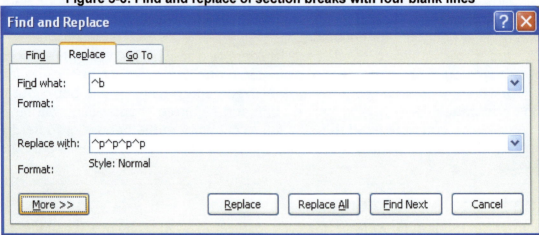

To make sure Word does the search correctly, make the breaks visible using the **Show/Hide** button ¶ (see 1.2) or change the view to **Draft** or **Normal** (see 1.7).

6. Editing

Microsoft Word includes a slew of tools that help during the writing and editing process. You probably noticed the built-in spelling and grammar checks, since the red and green wavy underlines shown in Figure 6-1 appear as soon as Word thinks you are wrong. The program also includes other tools such as a thesaurus, translation and hyphenation functions, a word counter, and a full-fledged group revision management system.

Figure 6-1: Passage with wavy underlines marking possible errors

Microsoft Word includes a slew of tools that help during the writing and editing process. You probably noticed the built-in spelling and grammar checks, since the wavy line appear as soon as Word thinks you are wrong. The program also includes othr tools such as a thesaurus, translation and hyphenation functions, a word counter, and a full-fledged group revision management system.¶

6.1.   *Spelling and Grammar*

Out of the box, Word checks spelling and basic grammar as you type and flags misspellings by red wavy underlines under the word. Green wavy underlines indicate grammar issues. Right-clicking on the flagged text brings up a pop-up menu with various choices.

Correcting spelling and grammar errors as you type

Right-click the text above the wavy underline
MAC: Hold down [Control] and click the text above the wavy underline.
Select replacement text from the pop-up menu.

At the top of the list is possible replacement text based on Word's best guess of your intentions. Clicking on any of the choices replaces the faulty text with your chosen alternative. At times Word offers a comment in grey, because it did not find anything. Since even humans do not agree on every aspect of a language, a computer program certainly cannot have all the answers either. Do further research on the phrases or check various style guides and take it from there.

If you are sure that Word incorrectly flagged text, pick one of the options to stop it from doing so again in this editing session. The **Ignore** or **Ignore Once** choices only suppress the wavy line at the current location. Select it if you deliberately misspelled something or ignored grammar rules, for instance, because a character uses faulty language. If the checker flags words missing from its dictionary, a common thing with jargon or unusual names, **Ignore All** will suppress the wavy line for all occurrences of that word during the current editing session. Since reopening the document will show the wavy lines again, for longer works add the word to a custom dictionary instead with the **Add** choice. Word will no longer flag that particular word. If you used a deliberate misspelling for a particular project, or you made a mistake adding a word, you can remove it from the custom dictionary later. You can also add words in bulk without going through the pop-up menu, or create custom dictionaries for a project, including ones for other languages.

Modifying a custom dictionary

Open a document in Word, if you have not already done so. A blank one will do.
AR: Click **File | Options | Proofing**.
O07: Click **Office | Word Options | Proofing**.
BR: Click **Tools | Options | Spelling & Grammar**.

MAC: Click **Word | Preferences | Spelling & Grammar**, then click the [Dictionaries] button. Click the [Custom Dictionaries] button to load a **Custom Dictionaries** dialog box similar to the one in Figure 6-2.

By default, only the standard Custom.dic is checked. You can add additional ones by pressing the [New] button.

Select a custom dictionary in the list.

Click the [Edit] button.

MAC: **Word for Mac** displays the custom dictionary as document in Word that you can edit as normal.

In **Word for Windows** proceed as follows.

To add a word, type it in the **Word(s)** field, then click [Add].

To delete words from the list, select them and click [Delete].

> **TIP** If you select a dictionary name in the list, Word displays its file path at the bottom of the **Custom Dictionaries** dialog box. The dictionaries are standard text files. You can copy lists of words separated by carriage returns into the file in bulk without going through the dialog box. To add an entire text file, for instance one downloaded from the Internet, click the [Add] button in the **Custom Dictionaries** dialog box.

Figure 6-2: Custom Dictionaries dialog box

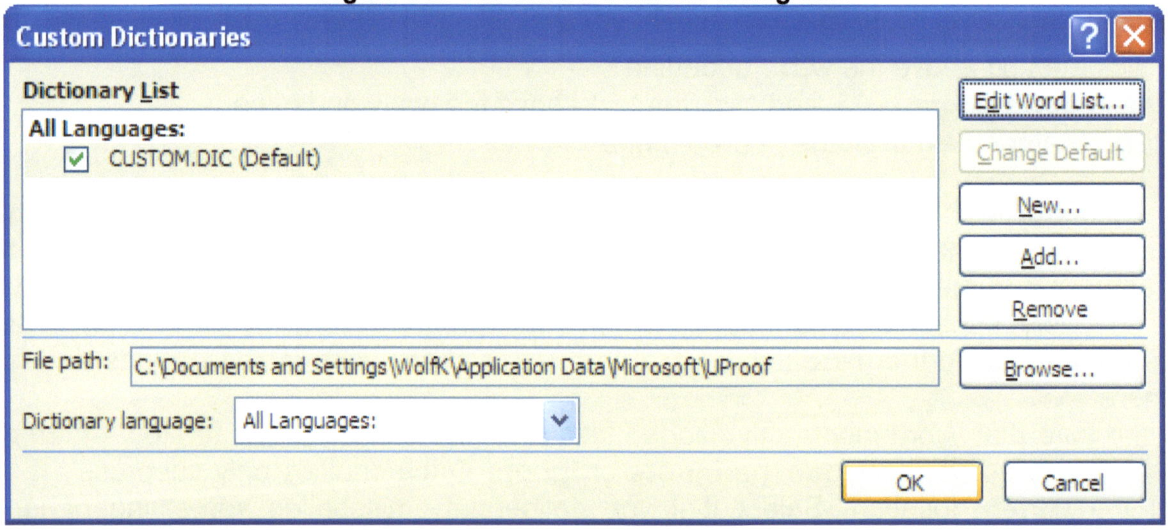

> **TIP** Words in the custom dictionary must match exactly. If you add countable nouns, also add the plural form with "s." If you add names of persons, also add the possessive with an apostrophe ('s). If you checked the AutoCorrect (see 3.3) option **Automatically use suggestions from the spelling checker**, Word will automatically correct any lowercase spelling of capitalized entries. If you have a need for both upper- and lowercase spelling of a word, other than at the beginning of a sentence, add both forms to the custom dictionary.

You can adjust some checking rules to your liking. By default Word ignores any words completely in uppercase, those containing numbers, and phrases that look like Internet or file addresses. It does flag repeated words such as "and and."

Changing spelling and grammar checking options

AR: Click **File | Options | Proofing**.
O07: Click **Office | Word Options | Proofing**.
BR: Click **Tools | Options | Spelling & Grammar**.

: Click **Word | Preferences | Spelling & Grammar**. Change options as desired.

If the wavy underlines bother you, you can run the spelling and grammar checker at your discretion by clearing **Check spelling as you type** and **Mark grammar errors as you type**. If **Use contextual spelling** is checked, Word will flag correctly spelled words out of context, such as using "their" for "there." Checking **Show readability statistics** shows them for the document after you finish checking spelling all at once as discussed below. If you write for a particular audience, such as children, the statistics help you gauge, if the text is at the appropriate grade level.

Changing the **Writing style** entry adds checks for writing style, in addition to grammar rules. Given the lack of agreement in style matters, Word lets you customize the rules in great detail. Click the [Settings] button to load the **Grammar Settings** dialog box shown in Figure 6-3, select a style option from the **Writing style** list as a starting point, then check or clear the options explained in the following tables. *You may find some options missing depending on your version of Word and language used.*

Figure 6-3: Grammar Settings dialog box

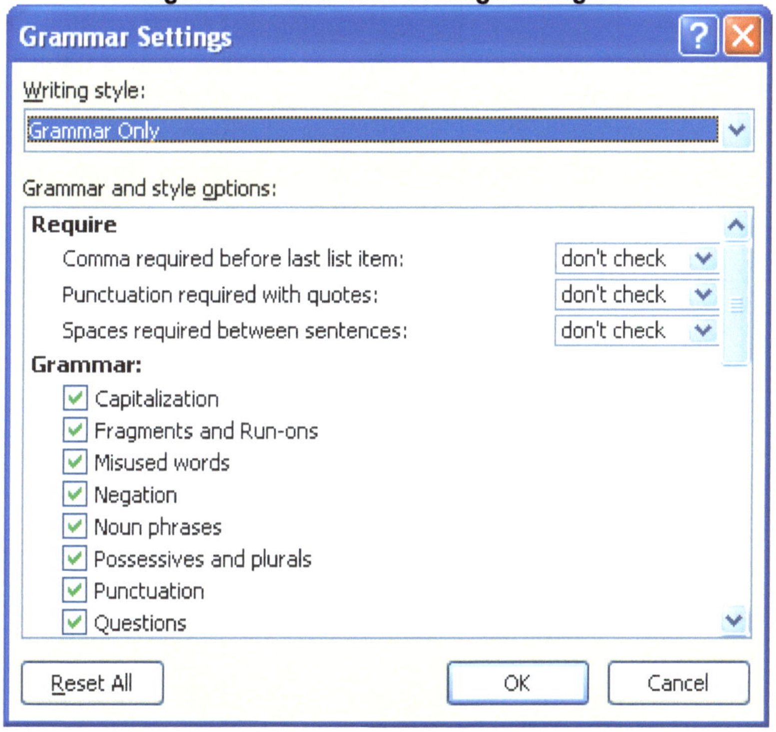

Table 6-1: Grammar options

Comma required before last list item	Whether a list of words separated by commas requires one before the "or" or "and."
Punctuation required with quotes	Whether punctuation at the end of a quote should be inside or outside the quotation marks.
Spaces required between sentences	Whether one or two spaces after an end-of-sentence punctuation separate sentences in the same paragraph.
Capitalization	Capitalization problems, such as known names or those preceded by titles. Also detects overuse of capitalization.
Fragments and Run-ons	Sentence fragments and run-on sentences.
Misused words	Various incorrect usage of words, for example, "like" as a

	conjunction, "what" versus "which," "who" versus "whom."
Negation	Use of multiple negatives, for example "I haven't never owed nothing."
Noun phrases	Incorrect noun phrases, particularly number agreement problems, for example a missing plural "s."
Possessives and plurals	Missing apostrophes in possessives or use of a possessive instead of a plural.
Punctuation	Incorrect punctuation, including at end of sentences, in quotations, use of a semicolon instead of a comma, or multiple spaces between words.
Questions	Incorrect use of question marks with non-standard questions, for example "Should we go to the party."
Relative clauses	Incorrect use of relative pronouns and punctuation, for example, "who" instead of "which," unnecessary use of "that."
Subject-verb agreement	Disagreement between the subject and its verb, for example, "Everyone are gone."
Verb phrases	Incorrect verb tenses or transitive verbs used as intransitive verbs.

Table 6-2: Style options

Clichés, Colloquialisms, and Jargon	Words or phrases listed as clichés in the dictionary; colloquialisms including "real," and "plenty" used as adverbs; "get" used as a passive verb; use of technical, business, or industry jargon.
Contractions	Use of contractions that should be spelled out or that are too informal, "He'd gone home."
Fragment	Use of fragments in formal writing, for example, "The dreaded SIS."
Gender-specific words	Gender-specific language, for example, "chairman" and "chairwoman."
Hyphenated and compound words	Hyphenated words that should not be hyphenated and closed compounds that should be open, and vice versa.
Misused words	Nonstandard words and word combinations, for example "ain't."
Numbers	Numerals under ten that should be spelled out or use of "%" instead of "percentage."
Passive sentences	Sentences written in the passive voice.
Possessives and plurals	Questionable possessive usages, for example, "He went to Chuck's."
Punctuation	Unneeded commas in date phrases, missing commas before quotations, and informal successive punctuation marks.
Relative clauses	Questionable use of "that" or "which."
Sentence length (more than sixty words)	Sentences that include more than 60 words.
Sentence structure	Sentence fragments, run-on sentences, overuse of conjunctions, nonparallel sentence structure, incorrectly formulated questions, and misplaced modifiers.
Sentences beginning with "And," "But," and "Hopefully"	Use of conjunctions and adverbs at the beginning of a sentence, or use of "plus" as a conjunction between two independent clauses.
Successive nouns (more than three)	Unclear succession of more than three nouns.
Successive	Succession of more than three prepositional phrases, for example

prepositional phrases (more than three)	"The book on the shelf in the corner of the library with the pink walls on the main highway was checked out."
Unclear phrasing	Unclear phrasing, for example "We need more scrupulous people."
Use of first person	Use of pronouns "I" and "me."
Verb phrases	Use of indicative verb forms where the subjunctive is preferable; split verb phrases; and passive verb phrases.
Wordiness	Wordy relative clauses or vague modifiers, redundant adverbs, or too many negatives.
Words in split infinitives (more than one)	Two or more words between "to" and an infinitive verb, as in "to very boldly go where no man…"

Checking spelling and grammar all at once

AR: Click **Review | Spelling & Grammar**.
O13: Click **Checking for proofing errors** icon in the **Status Bar**.
BR/MAC: Click **Tools | Spelling & Grammar**.

```
[F7] (or MAC: [Cmd] + [Option] + [L])
```

When done all at once, a **Spelling and Grammar** dialog box similar to the one in Figure 6-4 appears. It offers the already familiar options from the pop-up menu and a few additional ones. The [Next Sentence] button allows you to move on to the next flagged phrase without taking any action on the current one. The [Undo] button undoes the previous action, including clicking [Next Sentence]. The [Explain] button opens a help window with an explanation of the grammar rule violated. For spelling errors, [Change] applies the selected correction from the **Suggestions** list at the current location, whereas [Change All] applies it to all similar misspellings in the document. The [AutoCorrect] button applies the change and adds the wrong and right versions to the AutoCorrect (see 3.3) table so future typing errors are fixed automatically. The [Options] button loads the dialog box to change the spelling and grammar options discussed above.

Figure 6-4: Spelling and Grammar dialog box

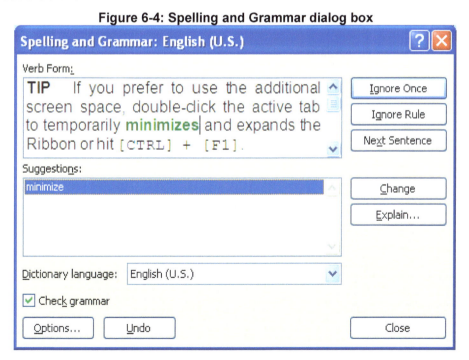

O13 Instead of the **Spelling and Grammar** dialog box, you now see a **Spelling** or a **Grammar Pane**. Explanations appear automatically in the lower portion. **AutoCorrect** is missing from the **Spelling** pane and the context menu.

6.2. Thesaurus and Dictionary

Figure 6-5: Windows and Mac Research task pane

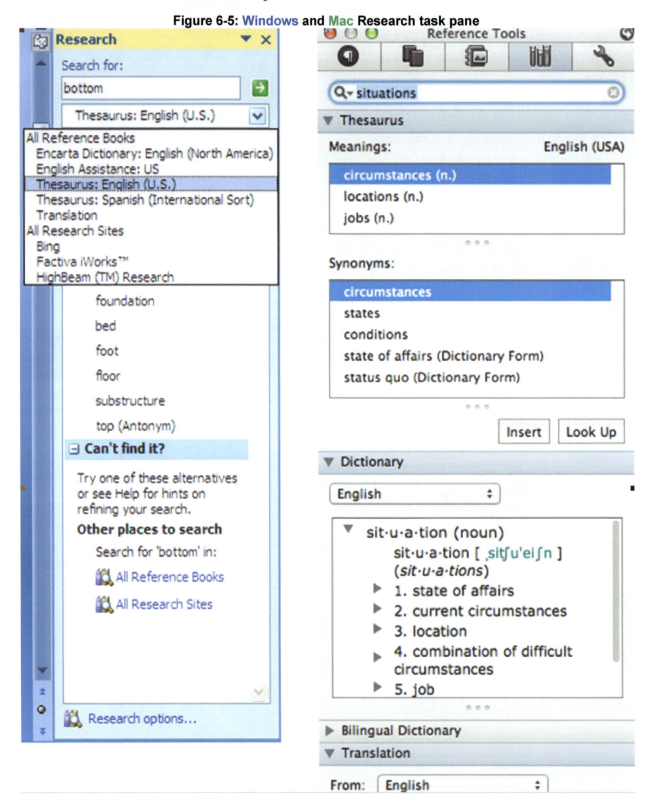

In addition to a customizable spelling dictionary, Word also includes a reference dictionary and a thesaurus. In its simplest form you right-click (**MAC**: [Control] + click) a word and select **Look Up/Define** or **Synonyms** from the pop-up menu. A definition or a list with alternatives appears. Clicking one of the synonyms replaces the word in your text with it. The simple list has its limitations, so the last entry is always the full-blown thesaurus, which loads the selected word into the Research task pane shown in Figure 6-5. You can select a built-in reference book from the list, or web sites. The [Research options] button at the bottom lets you add additional reference books and services by specifying an Internet address. Some dictionaries are *not* usable *without* an Internet connection.

Looking up a definition

AR: Click **Review** | **Research** (Proofing group).
O13: Click **Review** | **Define** (Proofing group) (*works only while on-line*).
BR: Click **Tools** | **Research**.
MAC: Click **Tools** | **Dictionary**.

[Ctrl] + [F7] (or **MAC**: [Shift] + [Cmd] + [Option] + [R])

Right-click a word and select **Look Up** or **Define**.

Looking up synonyms

AR: Click **Review** | **Thesaurus** (Proofing group).
BR: Click **Tools** | **Language** | **Thesaurus**.
MAC: Click **Tools** | **Thesaurus**.

[Shift] + [F7] (or **MAC**: [Cmd] + [Option] + [Control] + [R])
Type in a word and click the right-pointing arrow or click the [Look Up] button.

Right-click a word and select **Synonyms**.
Click **Thesaurus**.

> **O13**   To use a reference dictionary in Word 2013 you *must* download one first by signing into a Microsoft account.

6.3.   Translate

The **Research** pane also provides translation services. Look up the current word in one of the bilingual dictionaries or send the entire document to a translation web site.

Translating text

AR: Click **Review** | **Translate** (Proofing group).
BR: Click **Tools** | **Language** | **Translate**.
MAC: In Word 2011 click **Tools** | **Dictionary**, then expand the **Bilingual Dictionary** or **Translation** section.
Type in a word and click the right-pointing arrow or click the [Look Up] button.

Right-click a word and select **Translate**.

To send the document to the Internet translation service click the green arrow **Translate the whole document** or the link labeled **Translate this document**.

6.4. Hyphenation

For completeness, I will mention the hyphenation function that steps through the document similar to the spell checker and suggests word breaks to maximize the text displayed on a line.

Hyphenating text

AR: Click **Page Layout | Hyphenation** (Page Setup group).
BR: Click **Tools | Language | Hyphenation**.
MAC: Click **Tools | Hyphenation**.
MAC: Click **Layout | Hyphenation** (Text Layout group).

6.5. AutoSummarize

If you need a reason to hate the new **Fluent** interface, throw your computer against the wall, glue the pieces back together, and install an old version of Word, here it is. The AutoSummarize function is missing in Word 2007 and newer versions. Before Ribbon, you could tell Word to go through the document and pick out what it considered the most important sentences and reduce hundreds of pages down to as little as one hundred words. Like many of the language functions, the results were at times less than stellar, but the automated condensing still beat reading through the document and copying out key phrases by hand to build a raw synopsis that you can then condense down further. Those that never liked the crude summary, you can rejoice. Those that miss the function, find friends with a **BR** version of Word, e-mail them your document, and tell them to do the following.

Summarizing text

BR: Click **Tools | AutoSummarize**.
Word collects key sentences throughout the document and finishes by displaying the **AutoSummarize** dialog box.
Select whether to highlight the key sentences, paste a summary at the beginning of the document, or create a new document.
You can adjust the summary size by typing in a new **Percentage of original** value or selecting one of the preconfigured values from the list.

6.6. Word Count

A query letter should include the word count of the book or article. Rather than sit for hours counting words, unless you want to fall asleep, let Word take care of this boring task. If a word count is *all* that you desire, lower your eyes to the **Status Bar** and look for the **Words** field. Hunger for more? With a few clicks, you can get all the document statistics you never wanted to know about.

Generating statistics for a text

To limit the statistics to a part of the text, select it first.
AR: Click **Review | Word Count** (Proofing group).
BR/MAC: Click **Tools | Word Count**.

AR: Click **File | Info**, then click **Properties** and select **Advanced Properties**.

O07: Click **Office | Prepare | Properties**, then click **Document Properties** and select **Advanced Properties**.
BR/MAC: Click **File | Properties**.
Select the **Statistics** tab.

> **TIP**   The Before Ribbon **Status Bar** does not display a running word count, but the **Word Count** toolbar makes a decent substitute. Click **Tools | Word Count**, then click [Show Toolbar], or right-click the toolbar area and check **Word Count**.

6.7.   Track Changes

Sooner or later you want to give your work to someone else to review and mark any errors. In the olden days, writers would print out their manuscript double-spaced, mail it to an editor, and wait on pins and needles until the postal carrier returned with a stack of paper dripping in red ink. You can still do so, and the postal service will thank you for keeping them in business. In the day and age of e-mail and cloud computing, Microsoft Word offers faster, less error-prone alternatives. Given that my lousy handwriting qualified me to become a doctor, but I turned writer instead, I choose the electronic way, when I can, by turning on **Track Changes**.

Turning change tracking on or off

AR: Click **Review | Track Changes** (Tracking group).
BR: Click **Tools | Track Changes**, then click the **Track Changes** button on the **Reviewing** toolbar.
MAC: Click **Review**, then set the **Track Changes** switch in the Tracking group to **ON** or **OFF**.
MAC: Click **Tools | Track Changes | Highlight Changes**, then check or uncheck **Track changes while editing**.

```
[Ctrl] + [Shift] + [E]  (MAC: [Cmd] + [Shift] + [E])
```

After you enable change tracking, Word flags any changes to the document in the text or in the margins. Multiple writers can collaborate, provided they each have a distinct user name for Word. By default, Word assigns different colors for revisions made by the first eight authors. Hovering with the mouse over a markup displays a balloon help with the reviewer's name, the date and time the change was made, and the type of change.

> **TIP**   In the default setting each copy of Word assigns colors based on its view, so two reviewers looking at the same document could see different colors. You can assign a fixed color to your changes through the **Track Changes** options. For each **Color** box select the color that you want.

Determining the Word user name

AR: Click **File | Options | Popular**.
O13: Click **File | Options | General**.
O07: Click **Office | Word Options | Popular**.
BR: Click **Tools | Options | User Information**.
MAC: Click **Word | Preferences | User Information**.

AR: Click **Review |** *down triangle* ▼ under **Track Changes** (Tracking group), then select **Change User Name**.

O13: Click **Review** | *Clipboard dialog launcher* ⌐ (the tiny arrow in the bottom right corner of the **Tracking** group), then click [Change User Name].

Changing Tracking options

AR: Click **Review** | *down triangle* ▾ under **Track Changes** (Tracking group), then select **Change Tracking Options**.

O13: Click **Review** | *Clipboard dialog launcher* ⌐ (the tiny arrow in the bottom right corner of the **Tracking** group).

BR: Click **Tools** | **Options**, then select the **Track Changes** tab.

MAC: Click **Word** | **Preferences** | **Track Changes**.

MAC: Click **Tools** | **Track Changes** | **Highlight Changes**, then click the [Options] button.

BR: Click the **Show** button on the **Reviewing** toolbar, then select **Options**.

> **TIP**   The **Track Changes** options let you specify how inserted, moved, and deleted text is displayed, including replacing deleted text with the placeholders "^" or "#."
>
> **MAC**   In Word for Mac prior to 2011 a **Reviewing** toolbar appears, giving you access to the same options as the **BR** interface.

Unlike the line numbers, the markup often exceeds the size of the margins, causing a repagination. To suit different tastes and allow easy printing of a marked up document, Word offers four different views.

- **Final Showing Markup**, the default, shows insertions in the text in color, but removes deleted text to bubbles in the right margin.
- **Original Showing Markup**, shows deletions in the text in color and strikethrough, but displays inserted text in bubbles in the right margin.
- **Final** shows the document without markings as if all changes had been accepted.
- **Original** shows the document without markings as if no changes had been made.

> **O13**   These views changed to **Simple Markup**, **All Markup**, **No Markup**, and **Original**.

Switching change tracking views

AR/MAC: Click **Review** | **Final Showing Markup** (Tracking group).

O13: Click **Review** | **All Markup** (Tracking group).

BR: Click **Final Showing Markup** on the **Reviewing** toolbar.

> **TIP**   To display a printable shaded background in the right margin to separate the document text from the tracked changes, click **Review** | **Show Markup**, then select **Markup Area Highlight**.

The **Show Markup** button on the **Review** Ribbon and the **Show** button on the **Reviewing** toolbar let you turn on and off different categories of markings and limit the display to a selected author. The **Balloons** option forces all revisions as balloons on the side or inline. You can also look at lists of the revisions grouped by category by turning on the **Reviewing Pane** through its button on the **Review** Ribbon or **Reviewing** toolbar.

The real power of electronic tracking shows during revision time. Instead of searching paper pages for small colored marking, Word guides you from change to change without missing even a barely visible inserted comma, when you click the **Next** or **Previous** buttons on the Ribbon or toolbar. You can apply changes individually, or all at once.

Accepting or rejecting one change

Select a change with either the **Next** or **Previous** buttons, clicking on the markup in the text, or clicking the balloon on the right. To accept or reject multiple changes, select the text.
AR/**MAC**: Click **Review | Accept** or **Reject** (Changes group).
BR: Click **Accept Change** or **Reject Change** on the **Reviewing** toolbar.

Right-click a markup in the text or a balloon on the right, then select **Accept Change** or **Reject Change**.

Accepting or rejecting all changes at once

AR/**MAC**: Click **Review** | the *down triangles* ▼ under **Accept** or **Reject** (Changes group).
BR: Click the *down triangles* next to **Accept Change** or **Reject Change** on the **Reviewing** toolbar.
Select **Accept** or **Reject All Changes in Document**.

At times, a reviewer may want to call attention to a sentence or explain a proposed change. Word comes with a dozen highlighters to surround text with colored bands. Unlike the black or blue background visible when highlighting text through one of the *selection* methods (see 1.4), the color highlight is merely coloring. I use it to flag passages that need rewriting, for example repeated words.

Applying color highlighting to text

AR/**MAC**: Click **Home | Text Highlight Color** (Font group), or the *down triangle* ▼ next to the button to select a different color.
BR: Click the **Highlight** button on the **Reviewing** toolbar, or the *down triangle* next to the button to select a different color.
Drag the highlighter across the text to color it.
Click the button again or press [Esc] to turn off the highlighter.
If you select text *before* you click the button, Word colors the text and turns off the highlighter immediately.

> **TIP**   Use a light highlight color to print in black-and-white, or you will end up with unreadable grey bands.

Removing color highlighting

Select the text where you want to remove the highlighting
AR/**MAC**: Click **Home** | *down triangle* ▼ next to **Text Highlight Color** (Font group).
BR: Click the *down triangle* next to the **Highlight** button on the **Reviewing** toolbar.
Select **None**.

> **TIP**   To find color highlight in a document, open the expanded **Find and Replace** dialog box (see 1.6.1), leave **Find what** blank, click [Format] and select **Highlight**, then click [Find Next].

You can also insert comments attached to a word or phrase. Comments are marked with change information like other revision marks. Color highlights do *not* have such information.

Inserting a comment

Click a word or select the text to attach a comment to.
AR/MAC: Click **Review | New Comment** (Comments group).
BR: Click the **Insert Comment** button on the **Reviewing** toolbar.
Type your comment.

Changing a comment

Click a comment bubble and make any changes.

Right-click the marked up text associated with the comment, then select **Edit Comment**.

Removing a comment

Click a comment bubble or the marked up text associated with the comment.
AR/MAC: Click **Review | Delete** (Comments group).

Right-click a comment bubble or the marked up text associated with the comment, then select **Delete Comment**.

> **TIP**   Since comments do not print out, you can use them to attach related research to paragraphs. If you put character descriptions in comments, the **Reviewing Pane** gives quick access to them no matter where you are in the document. If you tag a crucial scene with a comment, you can jump to the page by clicking on the comment in the pane. This trick works with hidden text, so you can hide formatted character biographies or other long text at the end of the book and jump to the needed one through its comment.

7. Final Formatting

You've done it. You have typed your manuscript, edited, edited, and edited it again, used the dictionary, thesaurus, spell and grammar check, and tracked changes. All you have to do now is format everything for the printer or as an ebook. The following checklists help you with the finishing touches.

> **TIP**   Some steps require major changes to your document. Regularly make copies of the file so you do not lose all your work if you have to revert to a previous version. You can also turn on **Track Changes** (see 6.7) to allow you to reject errant changes.

7.1.   Formatting for printing

Most printers nowadays expect an electronic file formatted in particular ways to feed to their printing program. The following steps cover many of the critical areas.

7.1.1.   Create the final page layout

If you used standard letter size or A4 for your manuscript, but want to publish your book in a smaller format, you'll need to change the page size, and with it the page layout. Some publishers make templates available. To use them, copy the manuscript into the template—merging the styles if necessary (see 2.1.1)—and save it as a new file. Unfortunately, Microsoft Word resizes the page to match the source material for most paste options. Only the **Paste Special** option **Unformatted Text** reliably leaves the template's page layout intact, but you also lose any formatting like *italics*.

If pasting into a template messes up its page layout, change the properties of your source document to match the requirements of the publisher instead. Look at the settings of the downloaded template in the various dialog boxes like **Page Setup** (see 5.1) or **Modify Style** (see 2.2) and match them in your own document. If you already created sections, be sure to set the **Apply to** drop-down to **Whole Document** in the **Page Setup** dialog box when changing page size.

- If necessary, create a new paper size.
- Set the document's page size and orientation to match.

> **TIP**   The way printers work landscape pages may come out sideways. To avoid this issue leave the page orientation at portraits and create a page with width wider than height.

- Set **Mirror margins** and adjust the margin sizes as required, including a gutter on the inside of the page. Some printers require equal left and right margins and equal top and bottom margins. To allow trimming, the margins must exceed a minimum size, often 0.5 inches (1.27 cm).
- Change the header and footer **From edge** distances to ensure they stay on the page.

7.1.2.   Create headers and footers

If you have not done so yet, create the final standard headers and footers (see 5.2). Once you break the document into sections, you have to manage the headers and footers separately, so consider carefully, what you need. Most books can get by just fine with only a header if it includes the page number. Of course, if the footer only contains a centered page number, you can use the same one throughout the document.

- If you created headers or footers *before* you changed page size, you will need to adjust the tab stops (see 5.2) to have elements appear correctly centered or on the outside.
- If desired, create a standard footer with an appropriate style and a page number.

- Create a header with an appropriate style and a page number.
- If you follow the convention of having no header on the first page, check **Different first page**. Microsoft Word will remove the headers and footers from the first page. If you still want a page number in the footer, copy one from another page.
- If you want to have different headers on the odd and even pages or just want the page number on the outside edge of both pages, check **Different odd and even**. If you placed the page number on the right edge in the step above, Microsoft Word will generally flip the location for you if you selected **Mirror margins** above. If not, change the even header as needed. Many novels put the author name in the even header and the book name in the odd header. Anthologies or books with distinctly named parts usually have the book name in the even header and the part name in the odd header.

7.1.3. Modify the styles

Although print-on-demand programs are more forgiving than ebook conversion programs, the formatting may change in unexpected ways if you do not follow certain practices. Particularly, text centered with spaces may appear off if the program uses a different spacing than what you see on screen. Avoid these problems by using the built-in styles with proper paragraph formatting. Most, if not all programs, understand the *basic* Microsoft Word formatting.

If you used tabs and carriage returns instead of styles to format your text, you should convert it to the **Normal** style now, especially if you will also publish an ebook. Before you remove leading spaces, however, create a **Centered** style (see 2.3) if you have not yet done so. Next, search for any text with leading spaces or tabs and change those lines that should be centered to the **Centered** or **Title** styles. Only then remove any indents done with spaces and tabs and any blank lines done with carriage returns. See 2.1.1 for instructions to do this with **Find and Replace**.

> **TIP**   If you wrote your manuscript typewriter-style or in a bare-bones text editor and ended up with carriage returns after *every* line, you first need to remove all but those separating paragraphs. Depending on the formatting, **Find and Replace** can still save you much work and loss of hair. See my web site listed in the introduction for the detailed procedure.

If you used a publisher's template, the included styles may already have the right settings. Adjust any other ones as needed (see 2.2). Start with the **Normal** style. If the other styles inherit most properties from it, you will only need to change most settings once. Adjust the properties of the other styles as needed.

- Pick the desired font and size (**Font** choice in the [Format] button menu of the **Modify Style** dialog box). To avoid unexpected font substitution, stick with common fonts such as Arial, Book Antiqua, Bookman Old Style, Century, Courier, Garamond, Palatino, Tahoma, Times New Roman, Verdana, or Symbols. If you need unusual fonts, upload a PDF with fonts embedded instead of the Word version. This book, for example, was printed from a PDF.
- Set **Line spacing** to **Single** (**Paragraph** choice in the [Format] button menu of the **Modify Style** dialog box). If you want a blank line after every paragraph, under **Spacing** set **After** to the height of the font, usually 12 or 10 pt.
- Set **Indentation** and **Alignment** as desired (**Paragraph** choice in the [Format] button menu of the **Modify Style** dialog box). Commonly, the **Indentation** setting **Special** will be **First Line** and **Alignment** will be **Justified**. Set the **Left** and **Right** values for **Indentation** to 0".
- If you want to start a new chapter on a new page, set **Page break before** (See 2.1.2) in the appropriate **Heading** style. If you want the chapter heading prominently displayed below

the top of the page, set the **Spacing Before** value to a multiple of the font size, such as 40 or 48 pt. Due to possible unexpected results, do *not* use blank lines to force a new page.

7.1.4. Create front and back matter

In a book the pages preceding the body make up the *front matter*, or *preliminaries*. Some pages customarily lack page numbers, also known as blind folios, while others have lower-case Roman numerals. Each page is still counted, however. Notice that the introduction of this book starts on page iii, not i.

The change in page number format requires a section break (see 5.3) between the front matter and the body. Even if you only have one page of front matter, you must include a section break, since the body *always* starts with page number 1. Unlink the headers or footers of the body and restart its page number at 1 (see 5.4), then change the page number format of the front matter. If you have multiple pages with blank folios and additional pages requiring Roman numerals, add an additional section break between the two page groups, unlink headers or footers, and change the page number format without restarting page numbering.

Many authors now banish most of the front-matter items to the *back* or *end matter* that *follows* the body, rather than clutter up Amazon's "Look Inside!" sample pages with content that cheapens the appearance of the book or most readers find boring. The back matter follows the same rules as the front matter. After the body, create separate sections for items with page numbers and those without, unlink headers or footers, restart page numbering *at the page that would follow* the front matter, and change to Roman numerals. For consistency, you should use styles for the page numbers, headers, and footers in the front and back matter (see 2.3).

At minimum, your front matter should have a *Title* page with the title of the book and all author names as printed on the cover. Some people frown on preceding the names with "By." Avoid the derisive comments by leaving out the obvious. You can also include the *Colophon*, the technical information such as copyrights, edition dates, ISBN number, license terms, and publisher's web site, on the title page. Since both customarily have blind folios, combining them saves you from having to break the front matter into two sections, as you can use the **Page Setup** option **Different first page** to eliminate the page number in header or footer instead. For a more professional look, separate Title and Colophon page with a page break.

If you have a separate section with blind folios, include the following parts of the front matter.

- *Title*.
- *Colophon/Copyright*.
- If not included in the Preface page, a separate *Acknowledgment* page, to acknowledge those who contributed to the creation of the book.
- *Dedication*, where you name the people for whom you have written the book
- Any advertisements, for example descriptions of or sample chapters from your other books.

The remaining parts of the front matter belong in the section with Roman numerals.

- *Contents*, the table of contents consisting of the chapter headings with their respective page numbers. Include all front-matter or back-matter items with displayed page numbers. Try to keep the list to one page.
- *Foreword*, written by a real person other than the author of the book to give information related to the story, the writer, or changes made from previous editions.
- *Preface*, written by the author to tell how the book came into being, often followed by acknowledgments.
- *Introduction*, states the purpose and goals of the following writing.

- *Prologue*, narrative that sets the scene for the following story. Some consider it part of the body and number it as page 1.

Customarily three hashtags (###) mark the end of the body. The back matter then follows on a new page. Other than the Title and Contents, the previous items can also appear as back matter, in addition to the following.

- *Epilogue*, narrative that brings closure to the story.
- *Afterword*, the Foreword when placed in the back matter.
- *Author's Note*, the Preface when placed in the back matter.
- *Appendix/Addendum*, additional information to detail or update the information found in the main work.
- *Glossary*, alphabetized definitions of terms of importance to the work. Long works of fiction may list all characters and places in the story.
- *Bibliography*, a list of other works consulted when writing the body.
- *Index*, alphabetized list of terms with the page numbers where they can be found in the body text.
- *Blank*. Some printers require a blank last page.

TIP   In print publishing, sections generally start with an odd-numbered page on the right. To enforce this convention set the section break type to **Odd page** (5.3). Some versions of Word still show headers or footers on any preceding blank left-handed even pages. If this happens to you, you may need to add extra section breaks in front of these blank pages, so you can remove these headers or footers. Finish all pages first so you do not have to remove such extra sections later because the blank page moved to the right.

7.2.   Formatting for ebook

With ebooks the concept of page size goes out the window. Readers can change font size and line spacing to suit their needs, and the ebook device will reflow the text to match. Without a fixed page size, the concept of a page number for reference also goes out the window. Instead, you guide readers to different sections of the ebook with hyperlinks. If you have a manuscript formatted for printing, you need to create a separate version formatted for ebook as detailed in the following steps. The resulting file is then uploaded to a conversion service that creates a document in one of many ebook formats.

Each of these formats has its own special guidelines, particularly for handling page breaks. The notes follow the specifications used in 2014 by four major conversion services, EPUB 3.0 for **Kobo** and **Lulu**; **Kindle** MOBI Format 8; and **Smashwords** 1.14 for conversion to different formats including MOBI, EPUB, and Portable Document Format (PDF). Barnes & Noble's **NOOK Press** provides their own tool, Manuscript Editor, to do the final formatting. Many vendors such as **Apple iBooks** sell EPUB books but do not offer conversion services of their own. Kobo can convert a MOBI file to EPUB, and Smashwords can convert an EPUB file to other formats. If the results satisfy you, you can save yourself the effort of creating and maintaining multiple versions of your Word document.

TIP   Unless you are creating a PDF as part of the Smashwords conversion process, treat it like a printed book and format the document according to 7.1, except add hyperlinks as needed (see 7.2.8). Some PDF creation programs correctly convert them.

7.2.1. Create the final page layout

Since ebook devices ignore the page size and margins of your Word document, set them to standard values suitable for printing a PDF. Unfortunately, paper sizes differ from country to country, so whatever size you pick will cause problems for some customers. Whereas the most common size in the USA is letter, the most common in Europe is A4. If you created sections in the document, be sure to set the **Apply to** drop-down to **Whole Document** in the **Page Setup** dialog box when changing page size.

- Set the document's page size to Letter or A4 and adjust the margin sizes as required.
- For PDF printing, change the header or footer distance to ensure they stay on the page.

7.2.2. Modify the styles

Conversion services expect an electronic file to feed to their program, and unlike printers, the paragraph formatting must consistently use styles. Indenting or centering text with spaces may produce unexpected results. Avoid these problems by using the built-in styles with proper paragraph formatting. Most programs understand the *basic* Microsoft Word formatting.

> **TIP**   If you wrote your manuscript typewriter style with carriage returns after *every* line, you first need to remove all but those separating paragraphs. Depending on the formatting, **Find and Replace** can still save you much work and loss of hair. See my web site listed in the introduction for the detailed procedure.

If you used tabs and carriage returns instead of styles to format your text, you must convert it to the **Normal** style now. Before you remove leading spaces, however, create a **Centered** style (see 2.3) if you have not done so, yet. Next, search for any text with leading spaces or tabs and change those lines that should be centered to the **Centered** or **Title** styles. Only then remove any indents done with spaces and tabs and any blank lines done with carriage returns. See 2.1.1 for instructions to do this with **Find and Replace**.

> **TIP**   Some conversion services, eg Lulu EPUB Converter, do not recognize custom styles. You may have to use **Heading 1** through **3** for centering, or apply the formatting directly.

If you used a conversion service's template, the included styles may already have the right settings. Adjust any other ones as needed (see 2.2). Start with the **Normal** style. If the other styles inherit most properties from it, you will only need to change most settings once. Adjust the properties of the other styles as needed. Since many devices, like phones, have small screens, when in doubt err on the side of less white space to maximize displayed text.

- Pick the desired font and size (**Font** choice in the [Format] button menu of the **Modify Style** dialog box). Many ebook devices support only a limited set of fonts. Stick with the common ones such as Arial, Garamond, or Times New Roman, and modify any styles that use special fonts. To avoid odd wrapping of reflowed text, keep font sizes close together. Do not mix 12-point text with 20-point headers on the same page.
- Some ebook devices do not display colors and will convert them into shades of gray. Make sure that readers still get needed information. This book, for instance, uses dark color for different tip categories and identifies them with different tags. Do not use color to convey important information not obvious from the text, such as which character is speaking.
- Conversely, some devices allow multiple color schemes for background and text. For the **Normal** style, leave the **Font color** at **Automatic**. Do not set it to a specific color such as **Black**.
- Set **Line spacing** to **Single** (**Paragraph** choice in the [Format] button menu of the **Modify Style** dialog box). Some conversion programs remove what they consider excess carriage

returns. If you want a blank line after every paragraph, under **Spacing** set **After** to the height of the font, usually 12 or 10 pt.

> **TIP**   **Line spacing** of **at least at** or **exactly at** will produce overlapping text on ebook devices. Stick with the simple **Single** or **1.5 lines** and remove any value from the **At** field.

- Set **Indentation** and **Alignment** as desired (**Paragraph** choice in the [Format] button menu of the **Modify Style** dialog box). Commonly the **Indentation** setting **Special** will be **First Line** with a value between 0.25" and 0.5" and **Alignment** will be **Left** or **Justified**. Some services have problems with justified text. Try a conversion and check the results.

> **Kindle**   If you specify no indent, the Kindle will automatically indent the first line of each paragraph. If you want block text without indents, for the **Normal** style specify an imperceptible **First Line** indent of 0.01".

Ebook creation programs use the built-in Word style **Heading 1** (see 2.1.2) to find the beginning of chapters and create hyperlinks to them, for example from the table of contents. Readers demand this convenience, so publishers expect it. Amazon has gone so far as to remove ebooks from its store if readers complain about missing hyperlinks. Even if your chapter titles consist of nothing more than numbers, make sure they have the **Heading 1** style. Smashwords will identify the chapters if their titles start with "Chapter," but recommends the **Heading 1** style anyway. For Kindle Direct Publishing the style is required for chapters, whereas Lulu requires **Heading 1** for parts such as Title and Copyright and **Heading 2** for chapters, so just do it.

- If you want to start a new chapter on a new page, set **Page break before** (See 2.1.2) in the appropriate **Heading** style. If you want the chapter heading prominently displayed below the top of the page, set the **Spacing Before** value to a multiple of the font size, such as 40 or 48 pt. Consider, however, the space wasted on small displays.

Keep styles to a minimum. Unlike paper, ebook devices do not take kindly to constant changes in paragraph formatting. Some formatting choices such as block quotes do not work well on small screens. Convert problem styles to **Normal** or use one a with a different font to differentiate those passages.

> **TIP**   To convert all occurrences of one style to another, open the **Find and Replace** window (see 1.6.1) and leave both **Find what** and **Replace with** blank. Using [Format] set the style of **Find what** to the one you want to replace and **Replace with** to the desired style. [Replace All] will change all occurrences of the first style with the second one without changing any text.

Apply styles consistently. If you use multiple levels of headings, apply them in order **Heading 1**, **Heading 2**, and **Heading 3**. Use the **Outline View** (see 1.7), **Navigation Pane** (see 2.1.2), or **Document Map** (see 1.1.3) to check the organization of the document.

7.2.3.   Remove unsupported elements

Many objects Microsoft Word lets you insert do not display correctly in ebooks. Either remove them, or replace them with simple text or pictures.

- Most ebook formats do not support multiple columns for text or tables. Replace them with simple text, if you can. If you have to include tables in your ebook, take a screen capture of them, paste the images into a picture editor, save them as a JPEG JPG or PNG file, then insert them as inline images (see 7.2.4).

Taking screen captures in Windows

From the **Start Menu** select **Programs | Windows Accessories** or **Accessories | Snipping Tool**.

`[Alt] + [PrtSc]` (current window) or `[Shift] + [PrtSc]` (entire desktop)

Taking screen captures on a MAC

In **Finder** click **Apple** or **Go**, then **Utilities**, or press `[Cmd] + [Shift] + [U]`.
In the **Utilities** menu click **Grab**.

`[Cmd] + [Ctrl] + [Shift] + [3]` (entire desktop to clipboard)

`[Cmd] + [Shift] + [3]` (entire desktop to PNG file)

`[Cmd] + [Shift] + [4]` (selection to PNG file)

`[Cmd] + [Shift] + [Space]` (current window to PNG file)

The keyboard shortcuts save the image to a file on the desktop.

- Symbols, including bullet points and those in scientific formulas, may turn into question marks. Replace them with regular characters or insert them as inline images.
- Some conversion programs do not recognize Microsoft Word's bullet styles. If the bullets disappear, type in a simple symbol that many devices can display such as a dash (-).
- Ebook devices do not support the optional hyphens used to maximize text on print pages. Find and replace (see 1.6.1) every optional hyphens ^- with nothing.
- Ebook devices also have problems with floating text boxes used to position text or images on screen. Remove them. If you have many text boxes whose contents you need to save, consider third-party add-ins like Kutools for Word. If you must position objects with respect to each other, take a screen capture and insert it as a single inline image instead. Microsoft Word uses text boxes to position page numbers if you select an option other than in line with the headers or footers. Remove either the latter or the page numbers with their boxes.

> **TIP**   To locate text boxes use the **Navigation Pane** and search for **Graphics**. See 1.6.3. If you find a floating object or insert a new one, you can navigate easily to others, since all floating objects occupy a different layer from the text. `[Tab]` and `[Shift] + [Tab]` will move between these objects with two exceptions. These keys also move between parts of compound objects. You have to step through all of the parts before the keys will move to the next floating object. Headers or footers form separate layers, so you have to search these separately.

- For reflow to work right, the font size cannot change drastically within a paragraph. Obviously then, large, ornate letters at the beginning of a paragraph that extend across multiple lines (drop caps) cause problems. Replace them with first letters of only slightly larger size or in bold instead. Some authors instead use a style that has no indent for the first paragraph of a chapter.
- Without page numbers, the index becomes meaningless. Many ebook devices support search functions, so indexing loses much of its utility. You can create hyperlinks for each term, but keep in mind that *every* occurrence requires a separate, named bookmark. Save

yourself the work and delete the index at the end and all index field codes using the procedures in 4.4.

- Footnotes at the end of a page also cause reflow problems, so many services do not allow them. Place the text inline in parentheses or create endnotes with hyperlinks (see 7.2.8). I have posted macrocode for converting footnotes to text on my web site listed in the Introduction. You can convert footnotes in bulk to endnotes by selecting them, right-clicking the text, and clicking **Convert to Endnote**. Copy the entire endnote text to the body of the document. If you need to keep the pointers in the body text, use **Find** to search for them (see 1.6.1) and type in replacement numbers by hand.
- Ebook formats other than PDF do not use headers or footers. Even if they did, automatic page numbers will cause unexpected results. If you must include headers or footers, at minimum convert the page numbers to text (see 7.2.6) or remove them.
- Few devices can handle embedded multimedia files, such as audio or video. Remove them.

7.2.4.   Adjust images

Microsoft Word lets you go wild with images by providing an abundance of complex formatting choices. Unfortunately, most do not work for ebooks in formats other than PDF. Reflowing text prevents you from specifying exactly where a picture will appear on an ebook display. Text may not wrap correctly around floating images, those anchored to the *page* in a *separate drawing layer* independent of the text. Word considers any graphics object floating that is formatted other than **In line with text**. Devices treat any inline pictures like any other character and reflow them, so make sure the **Wrapping style** is set to that for every image. You may notice that with **In line with text** selected, the other positioning options are grayed out and unavailable as you want them. Since watermarks, pictures that appear *behind* the text, out of necessity have to float, get rid of them for ebooks other than PDF.

Setting picture wrapping style to **In line with text**

Click a picture.
AR: Click **Picture Tools Format** | **Wrap Text** (Arrange group)
BR: Click the **Text Wrapping** button on the **Picture** toolbar.
MAC: Click **Format Picture** | **Wrap Text** (Arrange group).
Click **In Line with Text**.

Right-click a picture and select **Format Picture**.
On the **Layout** tab under **Wrapping style** click on the icon above **In line with text**.
Click [OK].

Right-click a picture and select **Wrap Text** | **In line with text**.

> **TIP**   Use the **Browse** buttons or the **Navigation Pane** to find images in your document. See 1.6.3. Unlike **Browse,** the **Navigation Pane** *will* find floating images.

- If pictures are larger than the font size, Word adjusts the line height to match. Avoid unsightly breaks in the text wrapping by centering larger figures in their own paragraphs using an appropriate style.
- Some ebook devices do not display colors and will convert them into shades of grays. Keep it simple and use images that are recognizable at different sizes and shades of gray.

> **Lulu**   Lulu EPUB Converter does not handle CMYK (cyan, magenta, yellow, key black) images. You must convert them to the RGB (red, green, blue) format.

This book uses separate paragraphs without text and formatted with a style named **Figure** for stand-alone pictures that are mostly high-contrast screen captures. Embedded images, like icons, are sized to fit and **In line with text**, so they reflow with it.

> **TIP**   To get an idea of how an image will look in grayscale, **AR** click the picture and then click **Picture Tools Format** (MAC: **Format Picture**) | **Recolor** or **Color** (Adjust group) and hover with the mouse over **Grayscale**.

- Ebook devices cannot change the font or size of text embedded in images. Keep that in mind, if like in this book you have figures with annotated parts. Unless the device allows zooming of images, the annotations may become unreadable. If you can, remove any text from the image and type it into the document above or below the picture.
- Kindle Direct Publishing expects images as separate files from the text, and hence specifies that you save any images *pasted* into the body as separate files and *insert* them back into the text for best resolution—and hence best readability. Smashwords recommends the same process. Insert images in JPEG (.jpg or .jpeg extension) or PNG format with center alignment. If you create your own images, use the PNG format, if you can, as it produces better results than JPEG.

Inserting pictures

AR: Click **Insert** | **Pictures** (Illustrations group).
BR: Click **Insert** | **Picture** | **From File**.
MAC: Click **Insert** | **Photo** | **Picture From File**.

When you change the image file outside Microsoft Word, it does *not* update inserted pictures. To allow easy updating from within Word, click [Insert] and select **Insert and Link** (MAC: **Link to File** | **Save with Document**). You can select **Link to File** to minimize the file size of your Word document, but the pictures are *not* included when you send someone the Word file. You can get around that by sending a PDF file instead (see 7.3). Since Kindle Direct Publishing does not accept PDF, you *must* insert pictures before the conversion.

> **TIP**   Word **AR** will attempt to extract any pasted images into files when you save as web page. If you pasted many pictures, try this route first (see 7.3). If the result is acceptable, save yourself the tedium of reinserting all the images. Worst case you can insert the resultant files back into your Word document.

- While you have the image in a file, resize and crop it to the size you want. Although a picture formatted in Microsoft Word may look good on your screen, an ebook device may use the underlying image specifications instead. If an image looks the way you want right after you inserted it in Word without any adjustments, chances are it will look good in the ebook, too.
- You may also have to reduce the image size. Whereas printers prefer high-resolution pictures with 300 dots per inch (dpi) or more, most ebook devices have a much lower resolution. The high pixel density merely adds unneeded bulk to the ebook and slows the rendering process. If you inserted many high-resolution images, use Microsoft Word's compression feature to reduce them down to web/screen resolution of 96 dpi. *The process is irreversible.* Do *not* do the compression on the original of the document you use for print publishing.

Compressing pictures

Right-click a picture and select **Format Picture**.
On the **Picture** tab click [Compress].
Under **Change resolution** select **Web/Screen** or **E-mail**.
To compress all pictures at once uncheck **Apply only to this picture**.
Click [OK].

To compress all pictures at once click an image.
AR: Click **Picture Tools Format | Compress pictures** (Adjust group).
MAC: Click **Format Picture | Compress** (Adjust group).

7.2.5. Modify page and section breaks

Conversion programs handle page and section breaks differently. Check with your service on its requirements. Generally, though, since ebook devices do not display headers, footers, or page numbers, you do not need section breaks. Some programs will force a new page on soft page breaks, those created by Microsoft Word in heading styles. Other conversion services require manual page breaks, while others ignore both. The following steps create consistent breaks depending on the requirements of the program.

- To ensure that a new section starts on a new page, particularly for Kindle Direct Publishing, find and replace (see 1.6.1) every section break ^b with a manual page break ^m.
- If the conversion program does not handle soft page breaks correctly, insert manual ones (see 5.3) after every front matter page and every chapter.

> **TIP** If you used Word's automatic numbering in the headings to number chapters, you can find all occurrences of chapter titles with ^d autonum and use the replace text ^m^& to precede them with a manual page break, or ^p^p^p^p^& for four blank lines. If you did not use this feature, save yourself the trouble of adding the page breaks by hand and turn on numbering (see 2.1.2), do the replace, then turn it off again.

- If you want to use the same manuscript with multiple ebook formats, add carriage returns before and after the manual page breaks for those devices that use blank lines to separate chapters. Doing a find for ^m and replacing it with ^p^p^m^p^p will add two carriage returns before and after each manual page break. The find ignores soft breaks created by a heading style, so replace them with manual ones first as described above. The extra blank lines at the top of a page may create problems with some services such as Lulu, however.

7.2.6. Convert automatic numbers

At this point, you should have all the content you need at the correct location. We can now dispense with Microsoft Word specific automatic numbering. Many conversion services cannot handle the field codes used to number chapter headings or cross references. To allow ebook devices to display the correct values, convert them to text.

- If you only used field codes for dates, times, table of contents, or automatic numbering of chapter headings, you can convert all at once by selecting the entire document with [Ctrl] + [A] (see 1.4) and then using [Ctrl] + [Shift] + [F9] to unlink (see 4.2) all the fields in the selection, thus converting them to text. Once you exit Word, *this process is irreversible*. Keep a copy of the document with field codes, so you can make changes for future editions. Unlinking all fields does not convert hidden ones, such as index entries. If you have not removed them in 7.2.3, do so now.

- Unlinking also converts any cross references to text, thus taking away your ability to find them by searching for ^d ref. If you want to convert cross references to hyperlinks as discussed below, thus requiring you to edit each one anyway, do this before you unlink the rest of the field codes in bulk.
- If you also used heading and list styles for automatic numbering, you have to go through a second step, since Microsoft Word does not use field codes for them.

Converting automatic numbering styles to text

Open the Microsoft Visual Basic editor with [ALT] + [F11] (**MAC**: [Option] + [F11]). Click on the window inside the editor titled **Immediate**. Code in this portion executes the moment you press [Enter]. If the **Immediate** window does not show, select it under **View |** **Immediate Window** or hit [Ctrl] + [G] (**MAC**: [Cmd] + [Ctrl] + [G]).
In the **Immediate** window enter the following text.

```
ActiveDocument.ConvertNumbersToText
```

Press [Enter].
The code executes immediately against the active window, the one you were on when you pressed [ALT] + [F11], so make sure that is the document you want to convert.
Modify the styles to remove the automatic numbering (see 2.2).

7.2.7. Create front and back matter

As described under 7.1.4 you may need to add additional pages before and after the body. Unlike printed books, the author does *not* control ebook page numbers. The devices create them based on page size and user selected settings and do not use Roman numerals to distinguish between front matter, the body, or back matter. You do not need separate sections for them. Finish these parts before building the table of contents, so you can include them.

- The front matter before the body commonly consists of the Title, Copyright, Dedication, Acknowledgment, Contents, Preface, and Prologue pages in this order.
- Using a style like **Centered** or **Title**, center the book title, author names, copyright details, and dedication. Remember that many readers use small screens, such as smart phones, so resist the temptation to get cute with formatting. Since you do not control page size, you *cannot* vertically center titles. Any preceding blank lines waste precious screen space, so avoid them.
- Precede Preface and Prologue with a title using **Heading 1**, so they appear in the table of contents. If you have not done so yet, convert automatic numbering for your chapters to text first (see 7.2.6) and turn off the numbering in the style (see 2.2) before you apply it to Preface and Prologue.
- Mark the end of the body with three hashtags (###), then add the back matter with chapter titles using **Heading 1** style. To get as much of the body as possible into Amazon's or Smashwords' preview samples, many authors have banished much of the front matter to the end. Hence, the back matter commonly consists of the Epilogue, Afterword, Author's Note, Copyright, Dedication, Acknowledgment and advertisement pages. Since an ebook has no back cover, the back matter also usually includes the author's biography.
- Put manual page breaks or carriage returns after each of the above items to separate them depending on what the conversion service requires.

7.2.8. Build table of contents and other links

> **TIP**   Kobo Writing Life and the Lulu EPUB Converter automatically create a table of contents from the **Heading 1** lines during the conversion process, so you can skip this section.

Add a Microsoft Word table of contents without page numbers (see 4.3) before the first chapter of the body. If you included Preface or Prologue, the table of contents should precede them, too. If you converted an existing table of contents into text in step 7.2.6, insert a new one with hyperlinks.

- On a new page, create a centered title "Table of Contents."

> **Kindle**   Create a guide item by highlighting the title "Table of Contents" and inserting a bookmark (see 4.1) named toc. The Kindle automatically creates a Go To link to it.

- Insert a table of contents field.

> **Kindle**   Kindle will use a Microsoft Word table of contents as is and convert it to proper links.
>
> **Smashwords**   Microsoft Word uses hidden bookmarks for headings that give Smashwords grief. To create a useable table of contents convert it to individual hyperlinks (see 4.3) or text with [Ctrl] + [Shift] + [F9], create bookmarks with meaningful names, then edit the links in the table of contents to point to your bookmarks. If all your chapter headings start with the word "Chapter," you can also have Smashwords generate the table of contents automatically.

- For non-fiction, such as this book, you can add additional navigation links. Commonly authors link the chapter headings back to the table of contents or create separate "Top" or "Back to top" links common on web pages. The latter method has the advantage that you can copy the link to the end of every chapter instead of creating separate links out of each chapter heading.
- If you have cross references, such as the "see 4.1" below, you can link those to the chapter headings or create new bookmarks (see 4.1). Convert any automatically generated numbers to text (see 7.2.6).
- Convert endnotes pointing to a section at the end of the book to hyperlinks.

> **Smashwords**   To prevent multiple links to the same location showing up in Smashwords' table of contents start their bookmark names with "ref_."

- Do not place too many hyperlinks, as readers may accidentally land on them while paging through a book with their fingers.
- Test each hyperlink to make sure it points to the correct location. Hold down [Ctrl] and click the link. You can use [Shift] + [F5] to return to the location you started from. Use **Go To** (see 1.6.2) to check the bookmarks. The highlighted area should not extend over multiple lines. If it does, delete the bookmark, recreate it, then fix any hyperlinks pointing to it. Broken hyperlinks will jump to the top of the document. Although Microsoft Word hyperlinks are field codes with text, you *cannot* change the bookmark name in them by typing. Right-click the hyperlink and select **Edit Link**.

> **Smashwords**   To avoid problems with hidden Microsoft Word bookmarks, delete them after you have finished your linking. To see them, open the **Bookmark** dialog box by inserting a bookmark and check the **Hidden bookmarks** box. Highlight each one in turn and click [Delete].

7.2.9. Add a cover

For Kobo Writing Life, the Lulu EPUB Converter, or for PDF conversion insert your cover image as the first page of your document separated from the Title page by a manual page break. Resize the image to fill the page. For Kindle Direct Publishing and Smashwords MOBI or EPUB the cover is uploaded separately and integrated during the conversion process.

7.2.10. Perform a final review

Go through the following tasks to make sure no simple mistakes ruin the reader's impression of your precious book.

- If you used **Track Changes** (see 6.7), search for and accept or reject any remaining changes, then turn *off* **Track Changes** so no new markups are accidentally created.
- Run a final spell check for errors (see 6.1).
- Turn on **Show/Hide** (see 1.2) and look for any errant tabs ($\rightarrow$) or paragraph marks ($\P$).

7.3.   *Doing the Deed*

Update any remaining field codes before the final submission, particularly any table of contents or indexes with page numbers. Spot check that the pagination agrees with the body.

Microsoft Word text documents using only standard fonts usually cause no problems for printers. If you used non-standard fonts, or included many images, a printer may produce unexpected results. Creating a portable document format (PDF) file minimizes surprises. You can download and install many printer drivers that allow you to create a PDF by printing your Word document. If possible, select the options to embed all fonts and print in press quality or 300 dpi using the default full colorspace. If you have only black-and-white images, select the grayscale colorspace instead. Do not password protect the file. You may have to create a custom paper size to match the desired print size.

> **TIP**   Newer versions of Word include **PDF** as a **Save as type** under **File | Save As**. The default options work well for print publishing. You can override the options for fonts and images from the **Tools** drop-down menu.

Ebook conversion services usually do not accept PDF, but most will take a Microsoft Word document. Kindle Direct Publishing requires you to save the document as a web page with all images as separate files.

Saving a document as a web page with separate images

AR: Click **File | Save As** and set **Save as type** to "Web Page, Filtered."
O07: Click **Office | Save As**, select a folder, and set **Save as type** to "Web Page, Filtered."
MAC: Click **File | Save As** and set **Format** to "Web Page," and click on the button immediately to the left of **Save only display information into HTML**.
BR: Click **File | Save As** and set **Save as type** to "Web Page, Filtered.".
Select a folder and enter a **File Name**, then click [Save].

Open the resultant file in a web browser and check that everything still looks as expected. Microsoft Word may not correctly collect images in a folder. You may copy missing picture files from your original to the web page folder. If they still do not display, you will need to edit the image links to correctly point to the folder. Consult a web page design book for details.

You are now ready to upload the document to the publishing service. Many print publishers provide an on-line function to review the expected results, but since the screen does not translate to print one-to-one, you will not know for sure how your product looks until you get printed proof copies.

Conversion services for ebooks offer more instant gratification. You can use their free readers to check your product on various devices. The EPUB standards association makes available a free tool, ePubCheck, to verify that the ebook conforms to the latest standard. Various companies offer front ends to it. Adobe Digital Editions, a free tool available from the Adobe web site, and various browser plugins also let you check EPUB ebooks independently. Congratulations, you are done!

+++

One last Piece of Powerful Word Wizardry

To get you going quickly, this book, in a small number of pages, has covered a huge list of Word features useful to writers. Many options were only mentioned in passing. To keep the length reasonable, some less often used tasks did not make the cut. If I have whet your appetite for more, I will leave you with a powerful spell that will come in handy on your quest for knowledge and keep you from banging your head against the wall when problems arise.

Google

Substitute another search engine if you are not a Googler. The Microsoft and many other web sites contain a tremendous amount of useful information about the many features in the different versions of Word. User forums provide answers to almost any question imaginable, as long as you can formulate it correctly. This guide sticks closely to the terminology used by Microsoft in its online help and support web site, so using the same terms in a search query will most likely get you an answer to your question.

Now that you have graduated into the ranks of the Microwizards of Word, I will cast a vanishing spell, also known as the three hash tags that mark the end of a book, and disappear out of your life for now. Happy and productive writing. You have no excuse left not to create your masterpiece in Microsoft Word.

###

Index
Functions with their own section in this book are in **bold**.

www.ingramcontent.com/pod-product-compliance
Lightning Source LLC
Chambersburg PA
CBHW041419050326
40689CB00002B/579